THE ARAB-ISRAELI CONFLICT

Alex Woolf

FRANKLIN WATTS
LONDON•SYDNEY

Titles in this series:

THE ARAB-ISRAELI CONFLICT
THE KOREAN WAR
THE VIETNAM WAR
WORLD WAR I
WORLD WAR II: EUROPE
WORLD WAR II: THE PACIFIC

© 2004 Arcturus Publishing Ltd

Produced for Franklin Watts by Arcturus Publishing Ltd, 26/27 Bickels Yard, 151-153 Bermondsey Street, London SE1 3HA.

Series concept: Alex Woolf
Editor: Philip de Ste. Croix
Designer: Simon Borrough
Cartography: The Map Studio
Consultant: Paul Cornish, Imperial War Museum, London
Picture researcher: Thomas Mitchell

Published in the UK by Franklin Watts.

A CIP catalogue record for this book is available from the British Library.

ISBN 0 7496 5452 X

Printed and bound in Italy

Franklin Watts – the Watts Publishing Group, 96 Leonard Street, London EC2A 4XD.

Picture Acknowledgements:
All the photographs in this book, with the exception of those listed below, were supplied by Getty Images and are reproduced here with their permission.
Camera Press: page 33 (David Rubinger).
Topham/AP: page 36, 43, 44

ABOUT THE AUTHOR

The author, Alex Woolf, is an experienced writer and editor of children's information books, specializing in history and social issues at secondary level. His other books include *The World Wars: The Battle of Britain*; *Questioning History: Nazi Germany*; *Ideas of the Modern World: Fundamentalism*; *21st Century Debates: Terrorism*; and *World Issues: Genocide*.

CONTENTS

CHAPTER 1: THE FOUNDING OF ISRAEL

Jewish immigrants arriving in New York City, around 1920. During the early decades of the twentieth century, many thousands of Jews fled persecution in Europe to seek a new life in the USA.

The conflict between Palestinian Arabs and Jews began in the late nineteenth century, and intensified after the setting up of the Jewish state of Israel in 1948. The conflict is essentially about land and who controls it. The land in question is a small area on the eastern coast of the Mediterranean Sea, measuring about 26,000 square kilometres. The Jews have claimed that this land was promised to them by God, as stated in the Bible. It was also the historical site of the Jewish kingdoms of Israel and Judah during the first millennium BC. The Palestinian Arabs' claim to the land is based on the fact that they have lived there continuously for hundreds of years.

During the nineteenth century, there was a rise in anti-semitism (hatred of Jews) in many parts of eastern Europe and Russia, rooted in religious antagonisms and the perceived wealth and economic power of the Jews. From the 1880s, Jewish communities came under severe attack, and by 1914, some five million Jews had fled to new homes in the USA, Britain, Canada, Australia and South Africa.

Some Jews were worried that their people would never be safe from anti-semitism as long as they remained a minority in the countries where they lived. They believed that the Jews needed a homeland of their own. To that end, in the 1890s, a movement known as Zionism came into being. Zion was one of the hills of Jerusalem, the capital of the historical land of Israel. The Zionists wished to establish a new Jewish nation on the site of ancient Israel.

At that time, the land they wished to reclaim was known as Palestine and was governed by the Ottoman Empire, a Turkish empire that extended throughout the Middle East. In the 1880s, there were around 462,000 people living in Palestine, including 447,000 Arabs and 15,000 Jews. The Zionist movement led to a large rise in Jewish immigration to Palestine, and by 1914, there were around 60,000 Jews living there – about 10 per cent of the population. The Palestinian Arabs were unhappy about these new arrivals, and at times they clashed with the Jewish settlers.

In the late nineteenth century, Arabs throughout the Middle East began to develop an awareness of themselves as a separate nation, and there was a

The bodies of Jewish men killed in a campaign of anti-semitic persecution in the Ukraine in 1900.

HOMELAND

*'Palestine is our unforgettable
historic homeland.... The
Jews who will it shall achieve
their State. We shall live at
last as free men on our own
soil, and in our own homes
peacefully die. The world will
be liberated by our freedom,
enriched by our wealth,
magnified by our greatness.
And whatever we attempt
there for our own benefit will
redound mightily and
beneficially to the good of all
mankind.'*

[From *Der Judenstaat*,
Theodor Herzl]

**Jewish immigrants from Russia
work on a kibbutz in Palestine in
1912. Between 1880 and 1914,
over 60,000 former Russian or
eastern European Jews settled on
land in Palestine or worked as
hired labourers.**

**Palestine under Ottoman rule was divided into sanjaks, or sub-
provinces. (A wilayat is a province.) Between 1900 and 1918, Zionist
colonies rose in number from 19 to 47. The Palestinians lobbied their
Turkish leaders to end Jewish immigration and land purchases by
Zionists.**

growing movement to overthrow their Turkish rulers. By this time the Ottoman Empire was in decline, and the great powers of Europe – Britain, France and Germany – were looking for ways to extend their influence in the area.

The British government secretly made contact with Arab nationalist leaders in 1915-16, persuading them to rise against the Ottoman Empire, which was then an ally of Germany. In return, Britain promised to support the establishment of an independent Arab state in the Arab territories of the Ottoman Empire, including Palestine.

In 1917, the British government also announced its support for the establishment of a Jewish homeland in Palestine. The Balfour Declaration as it was known (after the British Foreign Minister, Arthur Balfour) contradicted Britain's earlier promise to the Arabs.

After the fall of the Ottoman Empire in 1921, the status of its former territories was discussed at a meeting of the League of Nations (an organization of countries established in 1919 to promote international peace and security). It was agreed that Palestine would be placed under British control. This was known as the British Mandate. Arabs were angry that Britain did not fulfil its promise to create an independent Arab state. They were also worried by the increasing numbers of Jews arriving from Europe. Clashes between the Arabs and Zionist Jews grew increasingly violent during the 1920s and 1930s. Jewish immigration to Palestine continued to rise, particularly after the anti-semitic Nazi Party came to power in Germany in 1933.

THE UNITED NATIONS PARTITION

After the Holocaust – the systematic extermination of nearly six million European Jews by the Nazis during World War II – Jewish demands for an independent homeland in Palestine grew much harder to ignore. The British authorities, faced with growing Arab-Jewish violence, and terrorist attacks against government buildings by Zionist militias, wished to end their mandate. In 1947, they requested help from

THE BALFOUR DECLARATION

'His Majesty's Government view with favour the establishment in Palestine of a national home for the Jewish people, and will use their best endeavours to facilitate the achievement of this object, it being clearly understood that nothing shall be done which may prejudice the civil and religious rights of existing non-Jewish communities in Palestine, or the rights and political status enjoyed by Jews in any other country.'

[From the *Balfour Declaration*, 2 November 1917]

T.E. Lawrence, better known as Lawrence of Arabia, a British army officer and champion of Arab nationalism who helped to organize an Arab revolt against the Turks during World War I.

British soldiers keep watch at Nablus, Palestine, in 1936. Between 1936 and 1939, British and Jewish targets came under attack during an Arab revolt.

United Nations (UN), an organization of countries formed in 1945 to replace the League of Nations

It was clear to all that the only way to resolve the Arab-Jewish conflict would be to divide Palestine in two. A UN-appointed committee proposed partitioning Palestine into two states, one Jewish, the other Arab. The division would ensure that each state would contain a majority of its own population. The Jewish state would control 55 per cent of Palestine. Under the plan, the disputed area containing Jerusalem and Bethlehem would become an international zone.

The United Nations partition plan of 1947. The Arab leadership claimed that it violated the rights of the non-Jewish majority in Palestine.

THE ARAB-ISRAELI CONFLICT

THE 1947-9 WAR Zionist leaders agreed to the plan, although they were unhappy not to be offered Jerusalem, a sacred city to the Jews. The Arabs rejected the plan. They believed the UN had acted under Zionist pressure to grant statehood to the Jewish settlers. On 29 November 1947, the UN General Assembly voted to accept the plan. Within days, military conflict erupted between Palestinian Arabs and Jews. The first phase of the fighting, which lasted until 1 April 1948, took the form of a low-level guerrilla conflict between small Arab and Jewish forces. There were no major battles, but numerous gunfights. Little territory was gained by either side. The British administration's authority had declined to such an extent that they were powerless to keep order, and simply let the two sides fight between themselves.

On 1 April 1948, Zionist forces took the initiative, and within weeks they had captured most of the territory allotted to them under the plan. On 15 May 1948, the British departed from Palestine, and Zionist leaders declared the founding of the state of Israel. Neighbouring Arab states – Egypt, Syria, Transjordan, Lebanon, and Saudi Arabia and Iraq which lay to the east of Transjordan – immediately invaded the new state. They did this, they said, to save Palestine from the Zionists. However, they also had ambitions to control parts of Palestine themselves.

The Israeli forces were fewer in number than their Arab opponents, but they were better trained and

The Arab invasion of May 1948, following Israel's declaration of nationhood. Jordanian forces launched an assault on Jerusalem, as Iraqi troops took up positions in various West Bank towns. Meanwhile, an Egyptian attack in the south wiped out a number of Israeli kibbutzim, and Syrian and Lebanese forces penetrated parts of northern Israel.

Israeli soldiers during the 1947–9 war prepare to launch an attack on Egyptian forces before capturing the Negev Desert in southern Israel.

organized. The battle was evenly balanced during the first two months of fighting, but when secret arms shipments began reaching Israel from Europe, the war swung in Israel's favour, and its forces began capturing territories beyond those granted by the UN partition.

The war ended when the UN arranged a series of ceasefires between the Arabs and Jews in late 1948. Armistice agreements were signed by Israel and the Arab states between February and July 1949. Under these agreements, former Palestine was divided into three parts: Israel controlled over 77 per cent of the territory (22 per cent more than it had been allotted by the UN); Transjordan took over East Jerusalem and the area known as the West Bank (this being the west bank of the River Jordan). Egypt occupied the coastal plain around the city of Gaza, known as the Gaza Strip. The Palestinian Arab state proposed by the UN partition plan was never established.

David Ben-Gurion, Israel's first prime minister, reads out the declaration of the founding of the State of Israel, in Tel Aviv, on 15 May 1948.

THE 1947-9 WAR

Start date:	29 November 1947
End date:	24 February 1949
Days	453
Total death toll	c.12,373

Combatants	Losses
Israel	6,373
Egypt	c.3,000
Syria	c.2,000
Jordan	c.1,000

CHAPTER 2:
THE SUEZ CRISIS AND THE SIX-DAY WAR

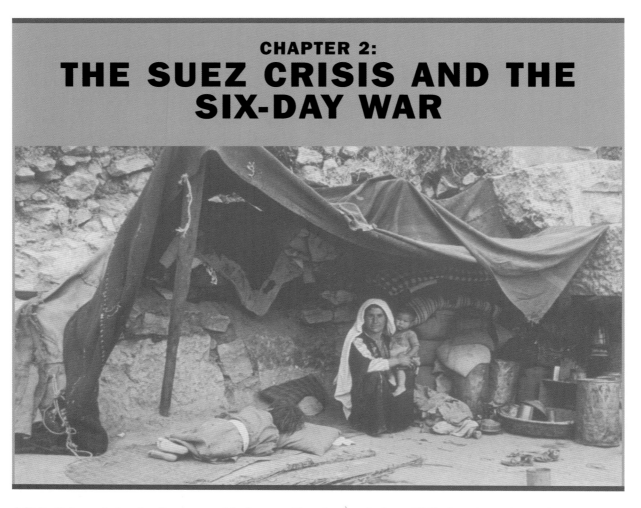

A Palestinian refugee family camp out in Amman, Transjordan, in June 1949. Despite a UN resolution recognizing the Palestinians' right to return to their homes, Israel barred refugees from re-entering Israel after the war.

According to UN estimates, the fighting in the 1947-9 war caused 726,000 Palestinian Arabs to flee Israel and become refugees. 470,000 moved to the West Bank (controlled by Transjordan, which in 1950 was renamed Jordan) and Gaza Strip (controlled by Egypt). 256,000 went to live in neighboring Arab states. Some 150,000 Palestinian Arabs remained in Israel, or returned to their homes during 1949. The reasons for the Palestinian exodus are disputed. Many Palestinian Arabs claim they were deliberately driven out by the Israelis. Israel says they were encouraged to leave by Arab government leaders.

An uneasy peace existed between Israel and the Arab states after 1949. Despite the signing of the armistice agreements, none of the Arab states

recognized Israel's new borders, or even its right to exist. Both sides began building up their military forces. The Soviet Union, originally a supporter of Israel, aligned itself with the Arab states, and began supplying them with military aid. The USA remained a supporter of Israel, although it did not begin supplying military aid until the 1960s. Israel acquired most of its weaponry from Britain and France.

THE SUEZ WAR The Suez Canal in Egypt was built in 1869 by a French company, Universal Company of the Suez Ship Canal, and the canal was jointly owned by the Egyptian and French governments. The canal, which ran through Egyptian territory, linked the Mediterranean and the Red Sea,

LEBANON
(13.5%–100,000)

IRAQ →
(0.5%–4,000)

Acre

Safed

Haifa

Tiberias

Sea of Galilee

SYRIA
(10.5%–75,000)

MEDITERRANEAN SEA

Beisan

Jordan

Jaffa

THE
WEST
BANK
(38.5%–280,000)

Ramla

AMMAN

JERUSALEM

ISRAEL

TRANSJORDAN
(10%–70,000)

THE GAZA
STRIP
(26%–190,000)

Dead Sea

Beersheba

0   25 miles

0   25 kilometres

EGYPT
(1%–7,000)

☐ Area from which Palestinians fled,
April–December 1948
● Towns with a large Palestinian population
← Direction of Palestinian flight
(1%–7,000) Percentage and number of refugees
reaching new areas

and was a vital trade route to the east. In 1882, debts forced Egypt to sell its share in the canal to Britain.

The canal continued to be jointly controlled by Britain and France until 1956. Early in that year, tensions between Egypt and Israel increased as Egyptians and Palestinians launched a series of border raids against the Jewish state, from Gaza. Israel responded with attacks of its own. In July, Egyptian leader Gamal Abdel Nasser nationalized (brought under national control) the Suez Canal. Nasser, who was a supporter of Arab nationalism, did not like the fact that European countries had power over a part of Egyptian territory. The tolls he could charge ships passing through the canal

The map shows where the Palestinian refugees fled, and roughly how many settled in each area. The UN set up an agency to care for the refugees. Today, more than 3.7 million Palestinians are registered with it.

Nasser arrives in the Egyptian capital, Cairo, in August 1956 following his announcement that he had nationalized the Suez Canal.

LIQUIDATION

'It is well-known and understood that the Arabs, in demanding the return of the refugees to Palestine, mean their return as masters of the Homeland and not as slaves. With a greater clarity, they mean the liquidation of the State of Israel.'

[Egyptian Foreign Minister Muhammad Salah al-Din quoted in *Al-Misri*]

THE 1956 SINAI CAMPAIGN

Start date:	29 October 1956
End date:	6 November 1956
Days	8
Total death toll	2,763

Combatants	Losses
Israel	231
Egypt	2,500
Britain	22
France	10

British paratroopers board an aircraft bound for Suez during the 1956 crisis. Britain and France began bombing Egyptian airfields on 30 October, then sent in troops on 5 November.

would also be a valuable source of revenue for Egypt.

By closing the Suez Canal to Israeli shipping and blockading the Straits of Tiran – another key trading route for Israel – Nasser strained relations between Egypt and Israel still further. He had also made enemies of Britain and France who had major economic and trading interests in the canal. A secret meeting took place between Israel, Britain and France, near Paris. It was agreed that Israel should invade Egypt, and that Britain and France would intervene

and ask the Israeli and Egyptian armies to withdraw from the canal zone. An Anglo-French force would then take control of the canal.

On 29 October, Israel invaded the Gaza Strip and the Sinai Peninsula, and advanced rapidly towards the canal zone. Britain and France, as previously agreed, offered to reoccupy the canal and separate the two armies. Nasser refused this request, so Britain and France launched a joint attack. However, before the invading forces could reach the canal, the USA put pressure on Britain and France to withdraw their troops. The US government was concerned about the damage their action might do to relations with the Arab states. It also feared the possible escalation of the conflict after the Soviet Union threatened to intervene on Egypt's side. The Anglo-French troops were pulled out on 22 December 1956.

French soldiers at Port Said, Egypt. After capturing this city, Anglo-French forces advanced to within 40 km of Suez City before the British agreed to a ceasefire.

The main routes followed by Israeli forces during their 1956 invasion of Gaza and Sinai. Israeli armoured divisions captured almost the entire territory by 5 November. The operation took just 100 hours.

Main Israeli advance routes, 29 October–5 November 1956

During the conflict, Israel captured both the Sinai Peninsula and the Gaza Strip, but in March 1957 it was forced by the UN to return to its previous borders. Israel failed to win back its shipping rights in the Suez Canal, but regained the freedom to use the Straits of Tiran. A demilitarized zone, policed by UN forces, was set up in the eastern and southern areas of Sinai, extending from Gaza to Sharm el-Sheikh, to act as a buffer between Israel and Egypt.

In August 1963, Israel began putting into effect its National Water Carrier Plan (NWCP), pumping water from the Sea of Galilee to irrigate south and central Israel. Syria, angered by this, readied its troops for attack. Israel did likewise. The UN persuaded both sides to pull back from conflict.

During 1964, the Arab leaders met at a series of conferences to agree joint strategies on how to deal with Israel. Several decisions were reached: they agreed to form the Palestine Liberation Organization (PLO) to represent the cause of Palestinian nationalism and help to unite Palestinians wherever they lived; they restated their intention to destroy Israel; and they

Levi Eshkol with his wife, Miriam. Israeli prime minister from 1963 until his death in 1969, the most significant moment of Eshkol's premiership was the 1967 Six-Day War.

The frontiers of Israel between 1949 and 1967. None of Israel's Arab neighbours recognized Israel's borders, or even its right to exist, at this time. From the mid-1960s, Syrian, Egyptian and Palestinian border attacks on Israel became more frequent.

decided to divert the Banias stream – one of the sources of the River Jordan, that feeds the Sea of Galilee – to prevent Israel from carrying out its NWCP.

Syria and Lebanon began work on the diversions in early 1967. Israel tried to block progress by firing on the tractors and earth-moving equipment carrying out the work on the Syrian side of the border. The Syrians responded by shelling Israeli towns in the north. Both sides began carrying out air strikes against targets across the border. As tensions escalated, the Soviet Union informed Syria that Israel was massing troops on the Syrian border in preparation for an invasion. The claim was untrue, but Syria did not know this, and called upon Egypt for help.

'THE ARAB PEOPLE WANT TO FIGHT'

On 15 May 1967, Nasser sent Egyptian troops into the Sinai. Three days later, he asked UN forces to withdraw from the demilitarized zone. The UN Secretary-General U Thant immediately complied with this request, and Egyptian troops were sent into Sharm el-Sheikh. On 21 May, Nasser closed the Gulf of Aqaba and the Straits of Tiran to Israeli shipping. Israeli prime minister Levi Eshkol interpreted this as an act of aggression against Israel.

Nasser's popularity rose in the Arab world; as in 1956, many were pleased to see him standing up for Palestinian interests by confronting the Israelis. On 27 May, Nasser announced, 'Our basic objective will be the destruction of Israel. The Arab people want to fight.' PLO Chairman Ahmed Shukhairy echoed these sentiments, saying it would be the PLO's privilege to strike the first blow; they would expel all the Zionists from Palestine who had arrived after 1917, and eliminate the state of Israel. Other Arab states were persuaded to join Egypt and Syria in committing themselves to war. On 30 May, Jordan signed a defence pact with Egypt, and on 4 June, Iraq did the same. Iraqi president Rahman Aref declared, 'Our goal is to wipe Israel off the map.'

The Israeli cabinet was divided on what to do about these threatening moves. Former prime minister David Ben-Gurion preferred to wait, while Moshe Dayan, a veteran soldier of the 1947-9 war, favoured an immediate attack on Egypt. The USA placed pressure

'...WITH ALL OUR MIGHT'

'We are engaged in defensive fighting on the Egyptian sector, and we shall not engage ourselves in any action against Jordan, unless Jordan attacks us. Should Jordan attack Israel, we shall go against her with all our might.'

[A message sent by Prime Minister Eshkol to King Hussein of Jordan on the morning of 5 June 1967. That afternoon, under pressure from Egypt, Jordan launched its attack against Israel.]

King Hussein of Jordan on a visit to a Royal Air Force base in the UK in 1966. Jordan signed a mutual defence pact with Egypt in May 1967, and took part in the 1967 conflict with Israel, losing control of the West Bank and Jerusalem in the process.

A map showing the Israeli advance on three fronts during the Six-Day War. An important element in Israel's success was its virtual destruction of the enemies' air forces, giving it air superiority throughout the war.

on Israel not to attack, but the mood in the cabinet gradually tilted towards aggressive action. Dayan was appointed Minister of Defence on 31 May. Menachem Begin, another supporter of war, was also invited to join the government. On 3 June, the cabinet was informed that the USA would not intervene if Israel went to war. The decision to attack was made on 4 June 1967.

THE SIX-DAY WAR Israel began its offensive at 7.45 am on 5 June 1967 with a surprise attack on the Egyptian air force. Egypt had the best-equipped and most modern of all the Arab air forces, but its airfields were poorly defended, with few anti-aircraft guns or armoured bunkers. The Israeli jets bombed and strafed the Egyptian planes and runways. In less than three hours they had destroyed virtually the entire air force

As well as destroying many Egyptian aircraft on the ground, the Israelis used tarmac-shredding penetration bombs on the runways, so that even undamaged planes could not take off.

on the ground, giving Israel air superiority for the remainder of the war.

Part of the Israeli Defence Force (IDF), consisting of three divisions, began to advance through the Gaza Strip and the Sinai Peninsula, encircling then defeating a powerful Egyptian force at Abu Aweigila. When Egyptian Minister of Defence, Abdel Amer heard that Abu Aweigila had fallen, he panicked and ordered all units in the Sinai to retreat. By 8 June, the Israelis had completed their conquest of the Sinai.

Nasser, desperate for help from Jordan, sent a message to its ruler King Hussein on 5 June in which he pretended that the Egyptians were winning their battle with the Israelis. Hussein gave the order to attack, and the Jordanian army began firing on Israeli positions in Jerusalem. Israeli forces counterattacked,

destroying the tiny Jordanian air force and encircling eastern (Arab-controlled) Jerusalem. On 6 June, an Israeli armoured brigade captured the West Bank towns of Ramallah and Jenin, and the following day they took control of Jerusalem's Old City and the West Bank town of Nablus. By 8 June, all of Jerusalem and the West Bank had fallen to Israeli forces.

From the start of the conflict, Syrian artillery had been shelling civilian targets in northern Israel from the Golan Heights, a 1,000-metre-high plateau on Syria's south-western frontier with Israel. On the evening of 5 June, Israeli jets destroyed two thirds of the Syrian air force, and forced the remaining third to

Israeli soldiers at Jerusalem's Wailing Wall – a holy place for Jews – following their capture of the Old City in 1967.

retreat to distant bases. The Israeli government was divided on whether or not to attempt to take the mountainous Golan Heights, a far more difficult operation than fighting on the flat desert of the Sinai. Levi Eshkol was in favour of an attack, but Moshe Dayan was against, concerned about fighting a war on several fronts. However, as good news poured in from the Sinai and the West Bank, Dayan warmed to the idea, and authorized the operation.

Early on the morning of 9 June, Israeli jets began bombing Syrian positions on the Golan Heights, and four Israeli brigades secured a base on the plateau from where they could be reinforced. On 10 June, the Syrian forces began retreating under heavy bombardment. By the afternoon, the IDF controlled the Golan

Heights, and was poised to advance on the Syrian capital, Damascus.

At this stage the Soviet Union, a firm ally of Syria, became alarmed. The Soviet premier, Alexei Kosygin sent a telegram to US president Lyndon Johnson,

Israeli units advance into Syria on 10 June 1967. During the assault on the Golan Heights, Israel lost 115 soldiers.

THE SIX-DAY WAR

Start date:	5 June 1967	
End date:	10 June 1967	
Days	6	
Total death toll	c.19,200	

Combatants	Forces (approx)	Losses
Israel	150,000 troops	776
	1,000 tanks	n/a
	200 aircraft	46
Egypt	100,000 troops	c. 10,000
	900 tanks	n/a
	385 aircraft	300
Jordan	60,000 troops	c 6,000
	300 tanks	n/a
	24 aircraft	20
Syria	50,000 troops	c. 2,500
	200 tanks	n/a
	97 aircraft	50

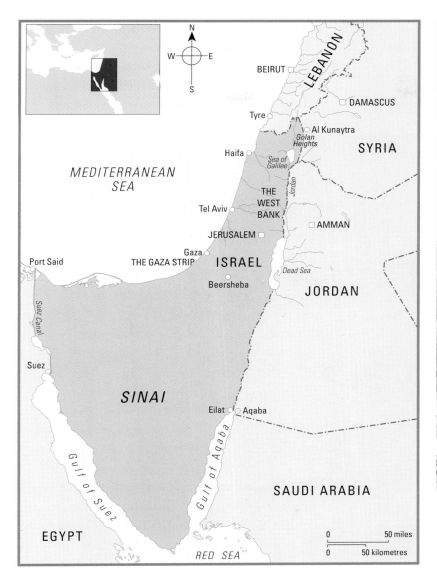

12 June 1967: Israeli troops salute their country's flag, now flying over the former Syrian territory of the Golan Heights.

By the end of the 1967 war, Israel had expanded its territory from 21,000 to 67,000 square kilometres. It would retain these new frontiers until October 1973.

threatening military action against Israel unless they ceased fighting in the next few hours. Both the US government and the UN urged the Israelis to stop their advance, concerned that this might develop into a far more serious confrontation. At 6.30 pm on 10 June, Israeli commanders ordered a ceasefire.

In the aftermath of the conflict, it was immediately clear that Israel had won a stunning victory. In just six days, Israeli forces had conquered the Gaza Strip, the Sinai, the Golan Heights and the West Bank, more than trebling its territory. Israel had inflicted a damaging defeat on its enemies, and established itself as the dominant military power in the region.

Israel had triumphed despite facing a combined Arab force that was greater in numbers and had more up-to-date weapons and equipment. Israel benefited from better leadership on the battlefield, superior training, and using tactics of surprise, speed and air superiority. The Israelis (many of whom had lost family members in the Holocaust of World War II) were also arguably better motivated, as most of them believed they were fighting for their very survival as a nation.

CHAPTER 3:
THE OCCUPIED TERRITORIES AND THE RISE OF THE PLO

An Israeli soldier stands guard at the new border with Jordan in June 1967.

Israel's conquests brought their own problems. After the Six-Day War, the Jewish state found itself ruling over more than 750,000 Palestinian Arabs, most of whom were hostile to their new government. Far from bringing Israel a greater sense of security, the 1967 victory only served to increase anti-Israeli sentiment among Palestinians and other Arabs. In November 1967, the UN gave its own verdict on the war, when the Security Council adopted Resolution 242, calling upon Israel to withdraw from territories it seized by force, and calling upon all the states to live in peace and recognize each other's (pre-June 1967) boundaries.

LAND FOR PEACE The Israeli government initially offered to return all of its new territories, except Jerusalem, in return for peace treaties with its Arab neighbours. The 'land-for-peace' offer was rejected by Egypt on 18 July 1967, and the following day it was withdrawn. Any further peace initiatives along these lines by the Israelis would be strongly opposed by elements within their own population. Religious Zionists had noted that the conquest of the West Bank, Gaza and the Golan Heights had brought Israel's borders roughly into line with those of the Biblical land of Israel. They were determined that these territories become a permanent part of Israel, and they lobbied the government to annex them and allow Jewish settlements to be built there.

In 1977, settlement expansion became official government policy, and increasing numbers of Jewish settlers made their homes in these areas. By 2003, 220,000 Jews had settled in the West Bank and Gaza, and an additional 200,000 had moved into areas of Jerusalem conquered in 1967. Some 15,000 Jews have settled in the Golan Heights, which was formally

RESOLUTION 242

In its Resolution 242, the UN Security Council called for: '*(i) Withdrawal of Israeli armed forces from territories occupied in the recent conflict; (ii) Termination of all claims or states of belligerency* [being at war] *and respect for and acknowledgement of the sovereignty, territorial integrity and political independence of every State in the area and their right to live in peace within secure and recognized boundaries free from threats or acts of force...*'

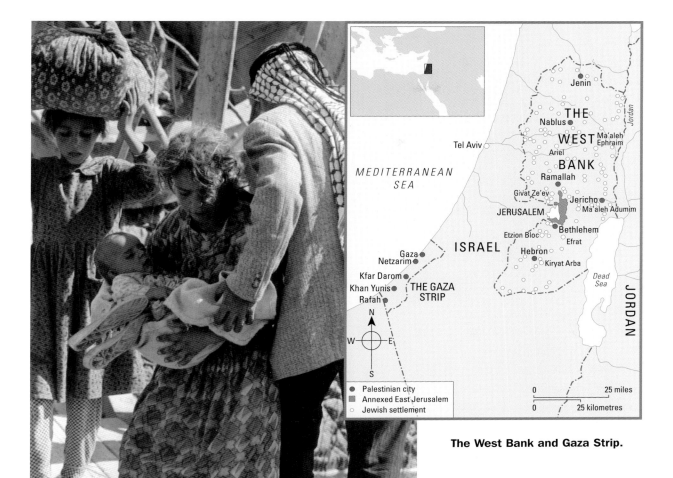

The West Bank and Gaza Strip.

Refugees cross between Jordan and Israel in 1967. Today, over half the three million Palestinians living in the West Bank and Gaza are refugees.

annexed from Syria by Israel in 1981. These settlements are in breach of UN Resolution 242, and have been a source of great anger and resentment for the Palestinian Arabs living in the occupied territories. Israel insists it has not broken international law with regard to the West Bank and Gaza Strip because they were not part of the sovereign territory of any state when Israel took them over. The territories (formerly part of the British Mandate) had been annexed by Egypt (in the case of Gaza) and Jordan (the West Bank) as part of the armistice agreement at the end of the 1947–9 War. However, they had never been internationally recognized as permanent parts of those countries. Therefore, Israel argues that it is not a foreign occupier, but a legal administrator of territory whose precise status remains to be determined.

From June 1967, Israel established a military administration to govern the Palestinians living in the West Bank and the Gaza Strip, which became known collectively as the occupied territories. Although Israel granted Palestinians living in the West Bank freedom of worship, in order to enforce security and counter terrorism there, Israeli authorities placed restrictions on the freedom of movement and freedom of the press for Palestinian residents of the occupied territories. Curfews were imposed, and roads, schools and community institutions were closed. Houses of suspected terrorists were demolished, and hundreds of Palestinians, accused of terrorist offences, were deported to Jordan or Lebanon, or imprisoned.

JERUSALEM Jerusalem has always had a special status because of its importance as a holy place to Jews, Muslims and Christians. The UN partition plan of 1947 advised that Jerusalem become an international city. The armistice agreed between Israel and Jordan after the 1947–9 war split the city in two: Israel took control of West Jerusalem while Jordan occupied East Jerusalem. East Jerusalem included the old walled city which contained religious sites important to Jews, Muslims and Christians. The city remained divided until 1967, when Israel captured East Jerusalem from Jordan, and then annexed it soon afterwards.

Unlike the military administrations of Gaza and the West Bank, Arab East Jerusalem was governed under Israeli civil law. The Israeli authorities redrew Jerusalem's boundaries, extending them northwards and southwards. Large Israeli settlements were established around the northern, eastern and southern boundaries of the city, creating a physical barrier between the Palestinian Arabs in East Jerusalem, and their countrymen living elsewhere in the

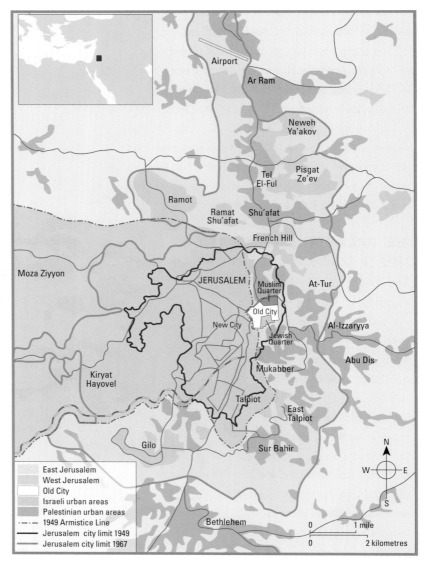

East Jerusalem
West Jerusalem
Old City
Israeli urban areas
Palestinian urban areas
- · - · - 1949 Armistice Line
——— Jerusalem city limit 1949
——— Jerusalem city limit 1967

A map of Jerusalem since the Israeli conquest of 1967. Israel annexed 10 square km of Jordanian Jerusalem and 103 square km of the nearby West Bank, renaming the entire area East Jerusalem.

Jews praying at the Wailing Wall in Jerusalem in 1973. Also known as the Western Wall, this is all that remains of the Jerusalem Temple, destroyed by the Romans in the first century AD, and regarded by Jews as the holiest place on earth.

West Bank. In 1980, the Israeli parliament passed a law making its annexation of Jerusalem official.

Jerusalem remains one of the most problematic issues in the Arab-Israeli conflict. Neither Israel nor the Palestinians agree with the UN plan to make Jerusalem an international city. Israel sees Jerusalem – the capital city of ancient Israel – as its 'eternal capital', and it is unlikely that an Israeli government would ever voluntarily give it up. Arabs regard East Jerusalem as part of the occupied West Bank, and want it to be the capital of a future Palestinian state.

THE CHANGING BALANCE OF POPULATION IN JERUSALEM

	Jews	Arabs
1948	100,000	65,000
1967	195,700	65,763
1984	346,700	126,100
1993	401,000	155,000
2000	454,600	215,400

An Arab Muslim passes two orthodox Jews in a Jerusalem street. On 27 June 1967, the Israeli parliament voted to give free access to Jerusalem's holy sites to people of all religions.

THE PALESTINE LIBERATION ORGANIZATION
The Palestine Liberation Organization (PLO) was founded in Egypt in 1964 to represent the large numbers of Palestinian Arabs living as refugees in Syria, Jordan and Egypt. In its early years the organization was controlled by the Arab nations who hoped to use it to advance their interests in the region. However, after the Six-Day War, many Palestinian Arabs lost faith in the Arab regimes, and began to build their own nationalist movements. One of these groups, called Fatah and led by a young Palestinian named Yasser Arafat, took over the PLO in 1967.

The PLO, now independent of the Arab regimes, became an umbrella organization for about eight different nationalist groups, each with their own views of how to achieve the ultimate goal of a Palestinian state. Arafat, as leader of the largest group, Fatah, became chairman of the PLO in 1969. The other major factions included the Popular Front for the Liberation of Palestine (PFLP), the Democratic Front for the Liberation of Palestine (DFLP) and the Palestine People's

Party (PPP). Despite their differences, most members of these groups – and the majority of Palestinians – regarded the PLO as their representative.

After the Six-Day War, some 400,000 Palestinians fled from the West Bank to Jordan. Here the PLO regrouped and decided to adopt terrorist tactics. From 1968, they embarked on a campaign of hijackings, and border raids into Israel from Jordan and Syria. On one occasion, in March 1968, a Jordanian-PLO force managed to inflict a rare defeat on Israeli troops at the town of Karameh in Jordan. The Israeli assault was launched after a terrorist attack left two Jewish schoolchildren dead. They were driven back by Palestinian guerrillas supported by Jordanian troops and artillery. The victory at Karameh won Arafat worldwide fame, and

One of the airliners blown up by the PFLP at Dawson's Field, Jordan, in 1970. This action led to the expulsion of the PLO from Jordan.

enabled him to recruit many more Palestinians to his cause.

In 1970, the PFLP blew up three passenger planes at Dawson's Field, a military airport in Jordan. By this time, the increasingly violent activities of the PLO were putting pressure on King Hussein, who felt that he was losing control of his own country. In 1970–71, the PLO were driven out by the Jordanian army, and forced into southern Lebanon. From this new base, the PLO continued to raid and shell northern Israel.

During the 1970s, the PLO began to alter its strategy. Worried by its terrorist image, it began to

seek international legitimacy as a government-in-exile. At the Arab League conference in Morocco in 1974, the PLO was officially recognized by the Arab peoples as the representative organization of the Palestinians, and in November of that year, Arafat was invited to address the UN General Assembly. The UN then granted the PLO observer status (entitling it to participate as an observer in all the sessions and debates of the General Assembly). To Israel's discomfort, Arafat had changed the image of the PLO from a group of ruthless terrorists to an internationally respected movement.

Jordanian premier Abdel Min'em Rifa'i with PLO leader Yasser Arafat (left) in 1969.

'SOMETHING HAD TO BE DONE...'

'The humiliation of having aircraft flown into Jordan and innocent passengers being whisked away to various parts of the country, and being unable to do anything about it, and having aircraft blown up, was something that questioned whether Jordan really existed. Well, that was the limit. As far as I was concerned, something had to be done – and done quickly.'

[King Hussein of Jordan on his decision to expel the PLO]

THE OCCUPIED TERRITORIES AND THE RISE OF THE PLO

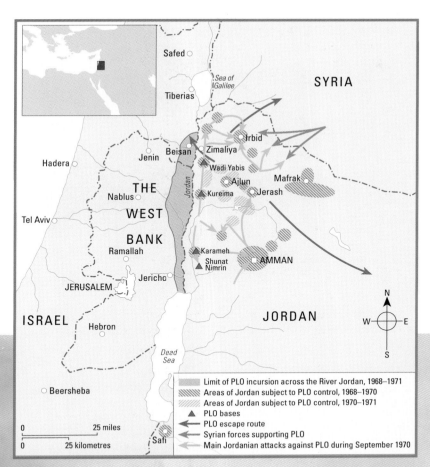

The map shows PLO bases in Jordan, and the conflict between Jordan and the PLO, which erupted in June 1970. At one stage, early in the battle, a Syrian tank force moved into northern Jordan in support of the PLO, but was forced to retreat.

Palestinian guerrillas, known as the fedayeen, patrol the streets of Amman during the PLO-Jordanian war. A ceasefire came into force in September 1970. However, sporadic fighting continued until Jordanian forces won a decisive victory in July 1971.

Limit of PLO incursion across the River Jordan, 1968–1971
Areas of Jordan subject to PLO control, 1968–1970
Areas of Jordan subject to PLO control, 1970–1971
▲ PLO bases
◄ PLO escape route
◄ Syrian forces supporting PLO
◄ Main Jordanian attacks against PLO during September 1970

CHAPTER 4:
THE YOM KIPPUR WAR AND CAMP DAVID

Artillery fire against Israel during the Yom Kippur War. The Egyptian-Syrian attack was well-supported, both militarily and financially, by other Arab states.

Soviet premier Leonid Brezhnev greets Anwar Sadat in Moscow in 1971. Sadat was seeking military support for Egypt from the Soviet Union.

From 1968, Egypt engaged in a series of low-level but persistent attacks against Israel in the Sinai Peninsula, aimed at wearing Israeli forces down. The cross-border confrontations grew increasingly intense until, under pressure from the US, both sides signed a ceasefire in August 1970, and declared their acceptance of UN Resolution 242. Shortly after this, Nasser died, and was replaced by a new leader, Anwar Sadat.

Unlike his predecessor, Sadat was genuinely interested in making peace with Israel. In February 1971 he announced that if Israel partially withdrew its forces from the Sinai, Egypt would reopen the Suez Canal and sign a peace agreement with Israel. By this time, Israel had a new prime minister, Golda Meir, who refused the Egyptian offer, despite pressure from

the USA to accept. Over the next two years, further offers of peace were also turned down. Israel, now receiving US military aid, felt itself to be in a strong position in relation to Egypt, whose forces had yet to recover to their pre-1967 strength.

Israeli plans to build a Mediterranean port near Rafah in Sinai, and its talk of creating settlements there, worried Sadat. He thought that the only way to

A map showing the lines of attack and counterattack during the Yom Kippur War. For the first four days of the conflict, Egypt and Syria made strong headway against surprised Israeli defences. However, after three weeks of fighting, the IDF was able to push the attacking forces back beyond their original lines.

recover this territory, and to lift Egypt's standing in the Arab world, would be to stage an attack on Israel.

THE OCTOBER WAR
On the afternoon of 6 October 1973, Egypt and Syria launched a joint invasion of Israel, code-named Operation Badr. They chose the day deliberately: it was Yom Kippur or the Day of Atonement, the holiest day in the Jewish calendar, and the Israelis were caught completely by

AIR ATTACK
'It was one o'clock in the afternoon, and I was driving my jeep to meet my commander. Suddenly I saw planes. I was very surprised. The Israeli air force flying on Yom Kippur! ... [then] I understood we were in a war.'

[General Amram Mitzna, Armored Corps, IDF]

surprise. Golda Meir and Defence Minister Moshe Dayan had believed that their forces in the Sinai were sufficient to deter any attack, and they dismissed intelligence reports that enemy soldiers were massing on their borders preparing to invade.

Huge numbers of Egyptian troops poured virtually unopposed across the Suez Canal and established a beachhead. A tiny force of Israelis manning the outposts along the canal were destroyed after offering limited resistance. Within days, Egypt had successfully reconquered the entire western bank of the Sinai peninsula. Israel's counterattacks on land and in the air were successfully repelled by Egypt's new Soviet-made anti-tank and anti-aircraft missiles. These missiles were neutralized only after Egyptian radar stations (which directed their strikes) were destroyed.

Meanwhile, to the north, Israeli defences, including just 170 tanks, were overrun by far greater Syrian forces (including 1,500 tanks and 1,000 artillery pieces) which penetrated deep into the Golan Heights and came within sight of the Sea of Galilee in northern Israel. During three days of desperate fighting, Israel's 7th Brigade managed to hold a line of rocky hills defending the northern side of their headquarters in Nafah (see page 27). However, the Syrians came very close to capturing Nafah from the south after destroying the Israeli 'Barak' armoured brigade. Israeli reserve forces arrived in time to prevent this, and swiftly counterattacked. By 11 October they had

THE OCTOBER WAR

Start date:	6 October 1973
End date:	22 October 1973
Days	16
Deaths per day	781
Total death toll	c.14,188

Combatants	Losses
Israel	2,688
Egypt	8,500 (approx)
Syria	3,000 (approx)

An Israeli armoured column advances into Syria on 17 October 1973. On that day, the Arab nations declared an oil embargo against the West for its support of Israel, which led to big petrol price rises.

reversed the Syrian gains, advancing to within artillery range of the Syrian capital, Damascus, just 40 kilometres away.

On the night of 16/17 October, General Ariel Sharon, commanding an Israeli division in the Sinai, disobeyed orders from his more cautious superiors, and crossed to the Egyptian side of the canal where he established a bridgehead between the Egyptian second and third armies. The IDF was able to cut off supplies to the Egyptian third army fighting in the peninsula, and Israeli forces came to within 100 kilometres of Cairo, Egypt's capital city. Israeli attempts to capture Suez City ended in failure. Under pressure from the USA and USSR, both sides agreed to a ceasefire on 20 October. A ceasefire was agreed with Syria on 22 October 1973, based on a return to pre-war borders.

After being caught so badly off guard, Israeli forces had managed a rapid recovery, and recaptured nearly all the territory they had won in 1967. Nevertheless, the war was a great shock to the Israelis, and losses had been heavy. They had underestimated the strength of their enemies, and had come very close to defeat. The Israeli government's lack of preparedness led to the resignation of Golda Meir and Moshe Dayan.

Occasional clashes continued across the ceasefire lines in the Sinai and Golan. The tension was only eased on 5 March 1974, when Israeli forces withdrew from the west bank of the canal, and Egypt

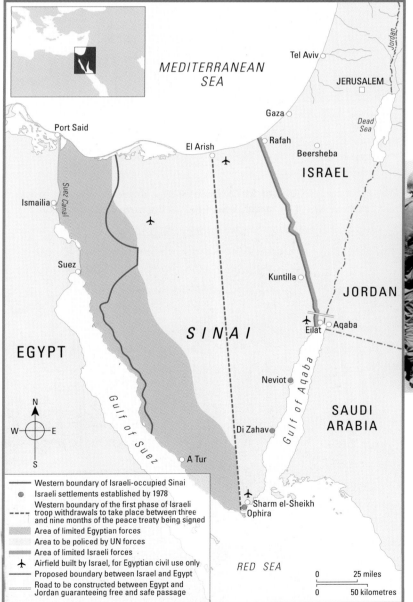

Map legend:
- Western boundary of Israeli-occupied Sinai
- ● Israeli settlements established by 1978
- --- Western boundary of the first phase of Israeli troop withdrawals to take place between three and nine months of the peace treaty being signed
- Area of limited Egyptian forces
- Area to be policed by UN forces
- Area of limited Israeli forces
- ✈ Airfield built by Israel, for Egyptian civil use only
- Proposed boundary between Israel and Egypt
- Road to be constructed between Egypt and Jordan guaranteeing free and safe passage

0   25 miles

0   50 kilometres

Following the end of the conflict, blindfolded Egyptian prisoners of war are led back to the western side of the Suez Canal, so they can return home.

The Sinai boundary changes agreed at Camp David (see p.30) in September 1978. Under the agreement, the Sinai would be returned to Egypt, but part of the territory would be policed by the UN as a security measure.

Begin (left), Carter (centre) and Sadat meet at Camp David in September 1978. The US president formed a relationship of friendship and mutual trust with Sadat, but found it harder to work with Begin.

took back control. On 31 May, Syria and Israel signed a disengagement agreement, and a UN peacekeeping force was established in the Golan Heights. Following the war, US Secretary of State Henry Kissinger tried in vain to negotiate an Arab-Israeli peace settlement by encouraging Israel to withdraw partly from the Sinai Peninsula and the Golan Heights. However, the US was successful in achieving a limited agreement between Egypt and Israel in September 1975 in which Israel withdrew most of its forces from the Sinai, and a UN-policed buffer zone was introduced between Egyptian and Israeli forces.

In November 1977, Sadat visited Jerusalem in an effort to secure peace between Egypt and Israel. He offered the Israelis permanent peace, and recognition of Israeli sovereignty, if Israel would withdraw from the occupied territories, including Arab Jerusalem, and agree to the establishment of a Palestinian state. Israeli prime minister Menachem Begin could not accept this, but did offer limited self-rule for the Palestinians in the West Bank and Gaza.

CAMP DAVID

In September 1978 US President Jimmy Carter invited Sadat and Begin to the presidential holiday retreat at Camp David in Maryland. Following twelve days of secret and often ill-tempered discussions, two agreements were signed. The first dealt with Egypt-Israel relations: both countries recognized each other, and the Sinai was returned to Egypt. This led to the Egypt-Israel Peace Treaty – the first between Israel and an Arab state – signed in March 1979. Israel completed its withdrawal from the Sinai Peninsula in 1982.

The second agreement tried to solve the Palestinian problem. It proposed giving Palestinians in

TOUGH TALKING

'I want you to understand that my right eye will fall out, my right hand will fall off, before I sign a single scrap of paper permitting the dismantling of a single Jewish settlement.'

[Menachem Begin speaking to US National Security Adviser Zbigniew Brzezinski about the Sinai settlements at Camp David]

Main PLO terrorist attacks
in Israel, 1976–8

Area occupied by Israeli forces,
15 March–13 June 1978

N
W E
S

MEDITERRANEAN
SEA

BEIRUT

LEBANON

Sidon

DAMASCUS

Tyre

Litani

SYRIA

Golan
Heights

Nahariya
6 November 1977, 2 killed

Haifa

Sea
of
Galilee

Jordan

11 March 1978, 39 killed

Tel Aviv

THE
WEST
BANK

AMMAN

JERUSALEM
1976, 8 killed

Gaza
THE GAZA STRIP

JORDAN

Dead
Sea

Beersheba

ISRAEL

0   50 miles

0   50 kilometres

SINAI

Eilat Aqaba

This map reveals PLO attacks on Israel (1976-1978), and Operation Litani, Israel's occupation of southern Lebanon (March-June 1978) which was undertaken in an attempt to strike back at the PLO.

occupied territories or the establishment of an independent Palestinian state. Israel also made the agreement more difficult to achieve by continuing to build new settlements in these areas.

OPERATION LITANI

Another reason for the failure to achieve an Israeli-Palestinian peace agreement in 1978 was the growing conflict on Israel's northern border with Lebanon. The arrival of the PLO in Lebanon in 1971, after their expulsion from Jordan, had caused tensions within the different ethnic communities of Lebanon – Muslim, Christian and Druze. Each sect had its own private army, and there were frequent clashes between PLO fighters and Christian militias in the capital city, Beirut. This led to a full-scale civil war beginning in 1975.

From 1976, PLO forces based in southern Lebanon engaged in a number of terrorist attacks on Israeli forces both in the occupied territories and in Israel itself. Following a PLO attack on a bus north of Tel Aviv, causing heavy casualties, Israel decided to attack PLO bases in Lebanon.

The invasion of southern Lebanon, known as Operation Litani, took place in March 1978. Israeli forces occupied most of the area south of the Litani River, which had been used as a base for anti-Israeli attacks. The UN Security Council responded by passing Resolution 425 calling for the immediate withdrawal of Israeli forces, and a UN peacekeeping force was set up in Lebanon. Israeli forces withdrew in June 1978, handing over positions along the border to a pro-Israeli force, a group of Lebanese Christian militiamen known as the South Lebanon Army. Israel was thus able to maintain a 20-km wide security zone to protect itself from cross-border attacks.

the occupied territories autonomy (self-rule) for a five-year period, after which time the final status of the occupied territories would be decided. This was rejected by the PLO and other Arab states because it did not guarantee full Israeli withdrawal from the

A street battle in Beirut during the civil war in Lebanon. Palestinian forces joined Lebanese Muslim factions in a fight against Christian militias based in east Beirut.

CHAPTER 5:
THE WAR IN LEBANON AND THE INTIFADA

Ariel Sharon, a key planner behind Operation Peace for Galilee, went beyond the original idea to attack PLO strongholds in southern Lebanon, and launched a full-scale assault on Beirut.

Despite Operation Litani and the establishment of a security zone, towns in Galilee in northern Israel continued to suffer attacks from PLO forces in southern Lebanon. To add to Israel's anxiety, Syria had become involved in Lebanon. In 1976 Syrian forces had moved in at the request of one of the parties fighting the civil war, a Christian sect called the Maronites, and Syria had used this as an opportunity to take over part of Lebanon for itself.

Tensions between Syria and Israel escalated further in April 1982 when Syria began positioning anti-aircraft missile batteries in Lebanon's Bekaa Valley. Israel saw this as a threat to its air reconnaissance activities over Lebanon. The Israeli government decided that another invasion of Lebanon was necessary to destroy both the PLO bases, and the Syrian missiles. Israel also wished to form a

partnership with the Maronite Christians; a Maronite government in Lebanon would – the Israelis hoped – be able to rid Lebanon of its Palestinian and Syrian elements. By mid-1977 the Maronites began to fear the growing dominance of their former allies, the Syrians, who were behaving increasingly like an army of occupation. The Maronite leaders were happy to form a new allegiance with Israel, the only force in the region powerful enough to confront Syria.

OPERATION PEACE FOR GALILEE

On 3 June 1982, an attempt was made to assassinate the Israeli ambassador in London. The Palestine National Liberation Movement was responsible, a rival organization to the PLO. Nevertheless, for the Israelis this was the excuse they were looking for to begin their invasion of Lebanon, which they named Operation Peace for Galilee. The invasion, planned by Defence Minister Ariel Sharon and Chief of Staff Rafael Eitan, began on 6 June. The Israeli army advanced into Lebanon, quickly overrunning PLO positions in the south, and reaching the outskirts of Beirut, Lebanon's capital and the headquarters of the PLO, by 8 June.

On 9 and 10 June, the Israeli Air Force (IAF) attacked and destroyed the nineteen Syrian missile batteries and their radar sites in the Bekaa Valley. The Syrian Air Force counterattacked, and a massive air battle took place, involving around 200 planes. The IAF inflicted a heavy defeat on the Syrians – who suffered from the lack of ground support – destroying

THE ISRAELI INVASION OF LEBANON

Start date:	6 June 1982
End date:	21 August 1982
Days	77
Total death toll	4,428

Combatants	Losses
Israel	368
PLO forces	3,000
Syria	600

Source: Martin Gilbert

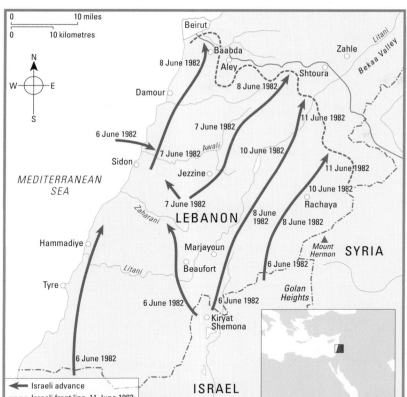

at least 87 of their aircraft, for the loss of around five Israeli planes. Under US pressure, Syria and Israel agreed a ceasefire on 11 June.

However, neither the USA nor the UN could persuade Israel to withdraw its forces from Lebanon. For two months, from 13 June to 12 August, the Israeli army besieged Beirut. The almost-continuous bombardment left 18,000 dead and 30,000 wounded,

During Operation Peace For Galilee, the Israeli forces advanced rapidly into Lebanon, overrunning PLO bases in towns like Sidon and Damour, before reaching Beirut just two days after crossing the border.

An Israeli tank on the streets of Beirut during the 1982 war. The IDF would sometimes strike at civilian targets if their intelligence informed them that PLO arms and munitions were hidden there.

A military convoy moves south across the Lebanese border as part of the Israeli withdrawal from Lebanon in 1985.

most of the casualties being civilians. Israel insisted that it would only end the siege when the 9,000-strong PLO force surrendered or left Lebanon, together with the Syrian forces stationed in Beirut. In August, US mediators succeeded in agreeing a ceasefire and the evacuation of PLO fighters from Lebanon. The evacuation began on 21 August. The PLO members moved to a number of different Arab countries, and the PLO leadership eventually settled into a new base in Tunisia.

Israel had succeeded in removing the PLO from Beirut, but had failed to neutralize the threat from

This map shows the Israeli troops in Lebanon pulling back to the Awali River on 3 September 1983. This was part of a staged withdrawal of Israel's military presence in Lebanon.

- - - - Israeli front line, September 1982–September 1983
——— Israeli front line, 3 September 1983

LEBANON

MEDITERRANEAN SEA

BEIRUT
Chouafat
Souk-el-Gharb
Damour
Aley Bhamdoun
Litani
Bekaa Valley
Deir el Kamar
Jebel Barouk
Sidon
Awali
Zaharani
Rachaya
DAMASCUS
Nabatiya
Marjayoun
Mount Hermon
Tyre
Litani
SYRIA
Kiryat Shemona
Golan Heights
Jordan
N
W E
S
Sea of Galilee
ISRAEL

0   20 miles
0   20 kilometres

RESPONSIBILITY

'It was only my allies, the Lebanese, who pushed me into leaving Beirut. Only when they told me, "Please, Arafat, this is enough ... what are you waiting for, Abu Ammar? Look, we are facing death from shelling and bombing from the sea, the land, the air ..." that I began to feel responsible for killing their children.'

[Yasser Arafat]

An Israeli soldier in Sidon, southern Lebanon. By 1984, heavy casualty rates and a lack of clear goals led many Israelis to question the wisdom of the invasion.

Syria, which continued to control 35 per cent of Lebanon. The Maronite Lebanese government – although sympathetic to Israel – was too weak to prevent Syrian-backed Lebanese and Palestinian factions from continuing to attack Israel. A peace treaty between Lebanon and Israel that called for Syrian troop withdrawals was signed in May 1983, but was cancelled by the Lebanese in March 1984, under pressure from Syria.

Many in Israel began to see the Lebanese invasion as a costly mistake. Over 300 Israelis had died in the operation, and hostile elements had not been defeated. Furthermore, Israel's international standing had been damaged by the invasion, which many saw as an unjustifiable act of aggression. There were anti-war demonstrations in Israel demanding withdrawal. In September 1983, the Israeli Army withdrew as far as the Awali River. In June 1985, Israel withdrew from most of Lebanon, but maintained an eight-km-wide security zone along the border, policed by Israeli troops

Palestinians throw rocks at Israeli tanks and soldiers in Ramallah on the West Bank in May 1988. The PLO later claimed to have organized the intifada, but it is more likely to have been a spontaneous uprising.

and members of the Maronite South Lebanon Army. Israeli forces finally withdrew completely from Lebanon in May 2000.

THE INTIFADA By the mid-1980s, the plight of the Palestinians had aroused a great deal of sympathy around the world, but their situation had remained largely unchanged since 1967: Israel's occupation of the West Bank and Gaza Strip looked set to continue indefinitely, new Israeli settlements continued to be built, and PLO leaders – now based in Tunisia – seemed powerless to prevent this. The anger felt by many Palestinians at their apparently hopeless situation was ready to boil over.

On the afternoon of 8 December 1987, an Israeli vehicle crashed into a car filled with Arabs queuing at a road block in Gaza. Four of the Arabs were killed, and by nightfall a rumour had spread through Jabalya – the largest refugee camp in Gaza – that this 'accident' had been a revenge attack for a previous killing. This was the spark that set off a mass uprising which came to be known as the *intifada* (meaning 'shaking off' in

THE INTIFADA

Year	Palestinians killed by Israeli security forces	Palestinians killed by Israeli civilians	Israeli civilians killed by Palestinians	Israeli security forces personnel killed by Palestinians
9-31 Dec 1987	22	0	0	0
1988	290	20	8	4
1989	286	19	20	11
1990	126	19	17	5
1991	96	8	14	5
1992	136	2	19	15
1993 (to 13 Sep)	131	7	22	20
TOTAL	**1,087**	**75**	**100**	**60**

[Source: http://www.btselem.org/English/Statistics/Total_Casualties.asp]

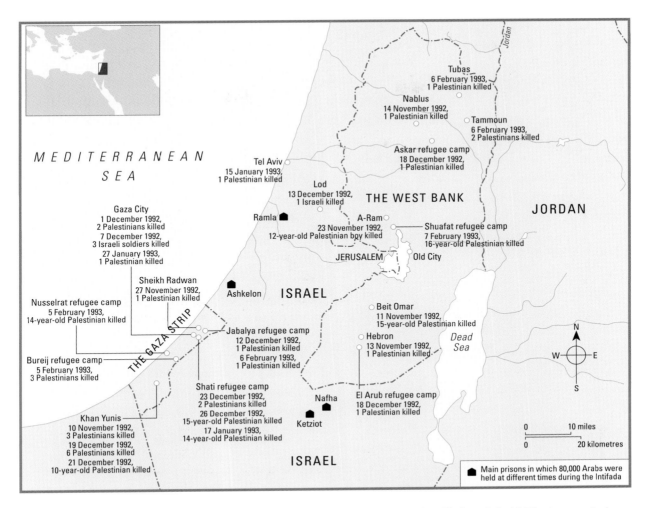

Tubas
6 February 1993,
1 Palestinian killed

Nablus
14 November 1992,
1 Palestinian killed

Tammoun
6 February 1993,
2 Palestinians killed

Askar refugee camp
18 December 1992,
1 Palestinian killed

MEDITERRANEAN
SEA

Tel Aviv
15 January 1993,
1 Palestinian killed

Lod
13 December 1992,
1 Israeli killed

THE WEST BANK

JORDAN

Gaza City
1 December 1992,
2 Palestinians killed
7 December 1992,
3 Israeli soldiers killed
27 January 1993,
1 Palestinian killed

Ramla

A-Ram
23 November 1992,
12-year-old Palestinian boy killed

Shuafat refugee camp
7 February 1993,
16-year-old Palestinian killed

JERUSALEM   Old City

Sheikh Radwan
27 November 1992,
1 Palestinian killed

Ashkelon

ISRAEL

Beit Omar
11 November 1992,
15-year-old Palestinian killed

Nusselrat refugee camp
5 February 1993,
14-year-old Palestinian killed

THE GAZA STRIP

Jabalya refugee camp
12 December 1992,
1 Palestinian killed
6 February 1993,
1 Palestinian killed

Hebron
13 November 1992,
1 Palestinian killed

Dead
Sea

Bureij refugee camp
5 February 1993,
3 Palestinians killed

N
W   E
S

Shati refugee camp
23 December 1992,
2 Palestinians killed
26 December 1992,
15-year-old Palestinian killed
17 January 1993,
14-year-old Palestinian killed

Nafha

Ketziot

El Arub refugee camp
18 December 1992,
1 Palestinian killed

Khan Yunis
10 November 1992,
3 Palestinians killed
19 December 1992,
6 Palestinians killed
21 December 1992,
10-year-old Palestinian killed

0   10 miles
0   20 kilometres

ISRAEL

■ Main prisons in which 80,000 Arabs were
held at different times during the Intifada

Arabic). Riots in Jabalya soon spread to Gaza City, and Nablus on the West Bank, and even into Jerusalem.

Unlike previous riots, the Palestinians were not deterred by the arrival of Israeli troops and armoured personnel carriers, but continued demonstrating and throwing bottles and stones. Gaza City streets were barricaded with stones and burning tyres, fiercely defended by Palestinian youths. Israeli forces hit back, killing 22 Palestinians and injuring hundreds more by the end of December. By that time some order had been restored with the introduction of road blocks, body searches and identity cards, but it was clear that the uprising had not been defeated.

While this first phase of the intifada was spontaneous, the next phase was planned. It was organized by different PLO groups – Fatah, the PFLP, the DFLP and the PPP – under the overall control of the United National Leadership of the Uprising

The locations of intifada-related killings reported between November 1992 and February 1993, when the violence intensified. As the intifada progressed, the weapons of the Palestinians changed from rocks to petrol bombs, grenades, guns and explosives.

(UNLU). Thousands of Palestinians were involved, including many who had no previous experience of resistance, such as women and children. The intifada involved different forms of resistance, including both violence and civil disobedience. As well as stone-throwing and the buiding of barricades, there were demonstrations, strikes, boycotts of Israeli products, and mass refusal to pay taxes.

Israel tried to smash the intifada with brute force. Between 1987 and 1991, Israeli forces killed 820 Palestinians and imprisoned some ten thousand others. By 1990, most UNLU leaders had been either killed or arrested, and the intifada had begun to run out of momentum, although it continued until September 1993.

The intifada failed in its main aim of bringing the Israeli occupation to an end. However, it succeeded in refocusing international attention on the Palestinian liberation struggle. It also shifted political power away from the PLO leadership in Tunisia (who had not started the uprising, nor played a significant part in running it) towards Palestinian groups based in the occupied territories.

THE GULF WAR

On 2 August 1990, Iraq invaded Kuwait, a small oil-rich country on its southern border. This act of aggression was widely condemned worldwide. A coalition of countries, led by the USA, was formed, threatening to take military action against Iraq unless it withdrew. The coalition included a number of Arab countries, including Saudi Arabia and Egypt. A large US military force began gathering in the Persian Gulf.

Iraq's leader, Saddam Hussein, cunningly attempted to split the coalition by linking Iraq's action to Israel's occupation of the West Bank and Gaza. He declared that he would only withdraw from Kuwait after Israel withdrew from the territories it had seized. In these circumstances, the PLO leadership felt they had no choice but to support Iraq. Arafat and Hussein released a joint statement saying they were united in their struggle against Israeli occupation and American intervention in the Gulf. Despite this provocation, the Arab states stood firm with the coalition, and Saudi Arabia and other Gulf states threw out a number of Palestinian activists. The PLO lost some international support for its stance. Palestinians, however, were inspired by Saddam Hussein's boast, and many saw him as a possible liberator of their people.

On 16 January 1991, the UN-imposed deadline for Iraqi withdrawal from Kuwait expired, and the coalition forces unleashed Operation Desert Storm – the removal of Iraqi forces from Kuwait by force. The occupation of Kuwait lasted just seven months before the coalition drove the invaders out. During the fighting, Israeli citizens were issued with gas masks because of the danger from Iraqi chemical weapons.

The remains of an Iraqi Scud, shot down by a Patriot missile near Riyadh, Saudi Arabia. A total of 46 Scuds were fired at Saudi Arabia during the Gulf War, while 39 of these missiles were fired at Israel.

US fighter jets flying over burning Kuwait oilfields during the Gulf War. Iraqi soldiers set fire to many of the oil wells in late February 1991.

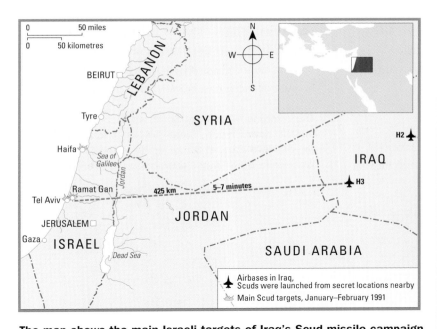

The map shows the main Israeli targets of Iraq's Scud missile campaign in January and February 1991 and the launch sites in western Iraq. Many Scuds were shot down by US-supplied Patriot missiles.

POPULAR RIOT

'It was clear that this uprising [the 1987-1993 intifada] *was on a new scale, and that these people were not "terrorists", but the population itself. There was a real threat that they might overwhelm the Israeli soldiers who were there in very small numbers. If they did, this would leave the soldiers with only two possibilities: to run away, or to shoot. … We were not technically prepared to deal with a violent popular riot on this scale.'

[Ehud Barak, Israeli Deputy Chief of Staff]

Parts of the occupied territories were placed under curfew in case the war sparked unrest in the Palestinian community.

On 17 January, Iraq launched eight Scud missiles into Israel, hitting parts of Tel Aviv and Haifa. Saddam Hussein's tactic was to try to draw Israel into the conflict, knowing that Arab countries would find it hard – if not impossible – to fight alongside Israel

against another Arab state. The US government gave Israel Patriot surface-to-air missiles to counter the Scuds, and urged Israel not to respond to the attack. The Scud attacks increased popular Palestinian support for Saddam, the first Arab leader to match words with deeds, and attack Israel's heartland. Israel suffered further Scud strikes, but did not hit back, and it won a lot of international sympathy for its restraint.

CHAPTER 6:
THE PEACE PROCESS

When he became prime minister in 1988, Yitzhak Shamir had a reputation as a hardliner, having opposed the 1979 peace treaty with Egypt. Yet he was prepared to let the Israeli government take part in the 1991 Madrid peace talks.

By November 1988, the intifada was almost a year old, yet the Palestinians seemed no further along the road towards independence. Palestinian activists in the occupied territories asked the PLO leadership in Tunisia to give a clearer political framework to their struggle. In response to this, the PLO made a number of key decisions: it agreed to recognize the state of Israel; it declared an independent Palestinian state in the West Bank and the Gaza Strip; and it renounced terrorism.

Israel failed to respond to this gesture. To Israel, the PLO remained a terrorist organization with which it refused to negotiate. However, two events in 1991 served to help the cause of peace. Firstly, with the collapse of the Soviet Union, Arab states such as Syria

and Egypt lost a key supporter, and so they had to be more accommodating in their dealings with Israel's most powerful ally, the USA. Secondly, following the Gulf War, the USA felt grateful for the support of the Arab states, and in return was willing to promote a settlement to the Arab-Israeli conflict, if necessary by putting pressure on Israel.

THE MADRID CONFERENCE
In October 1991, the USA organized a peace conference in Madrid, Spain, with the aim of resolving the long-running conflict. Israel, Syria, Lebanon, Jordan and the Palestinians were invited. It was the first time Israel had entered into direct negotiations with any of these states. Israeli prime minister Yitzhak Shamir insisted that the PLO must be left out of the talks, and the Palestinians were represented by a delegation from the occupied territories. However, the delegation was guided by PLO leaders staying in nearby hotels.

The talks consisted of both bilateral negotiations between Israel and each Arab state, and multilateral negotiations dealing with issues concerning the whole Middle East, such as water, arms control, economic development and refugees. The discussions which began in Madrid continued over the next three years in different places around the world. The Israel-Jordan talks resulted in the signing of a peace treaty between the two states in October 1994.

Despite numerous meetings between the Israeli and Palestinian delegations at Madrid, little progress was made. Further talks were held in Washington in mid-1992 following the election of a new Israeli government headed by Yitzhak Rabin. However, by

ENOUGH
'We who have come from a land where parents bury their children, we who have fought against you, the Palestinians, say to you today in a loud and clear voice, enough of bloodshed and tears. Enough.'
[Yitzhak Rabin, Israeli PM, before the signing of the Oslo Accords, 13 September 1993]

The agreed boundary between Israel and Jordan following the 1994 peace treaty. The treaty confirmed that each country could obtain their fair share of water from the Jordan River.

The fall of the Berlin Wall on 9 November 1989 (pictured here) and the end of the Cold War marked the beginning of a new drive towards peace in the Middle East as former Cold War rivals, Russia and the USA, placed pressure on Israel and the Arab nations to negotiate.

December these talks had also become bogged down. The slow pace of negotiations made people in the occupied territories impatient, and this led to renewed violence. Chiefly responsible for this new wave of terrorism were Islamist (strict Islamic) groups such as Hamas and Islamic Jihad, who had started to offer Palestinians a popular and radical alternative to the secular (non-religious) PLO.

THE OSLO ACCORDS
In mid-1992, a series of secret, informal talks began in Oslo, Norway,

Yitzhak Rabin (left) shakes hands with Yasser Arafat at the signing ceremony in September 1993 of the Oslo Accords at the White House, Washington DC. President Bill Clinton looks on.

PALESTINIANS AND ISRAELIS KILLED IN ISRAEL AND THE OCCUPIED TERRITORIES
(14 SEPTEMBER 1993–28 SEPTEMBER 2000)

Year	Palestinians killed by Israeli security forces	Palestinians killed by Israeli civilians	Israeli civilians killed by Palestinians	Israeli security forces personnel killed by Palestinians
1993	165	15	36	25
1994	113	39	58	16
1995	42	3	16	30
1996	69	5	41	34
1997	18	3	29	0
1998	21	7	9	3
1999	9	0	2	2
2000	14	0	2	1
TOTAL	**451**	**72**	**193**	**111**

[Source: B'tselem, the Israeli Information Center for Human Rights in the Occupied Territories]

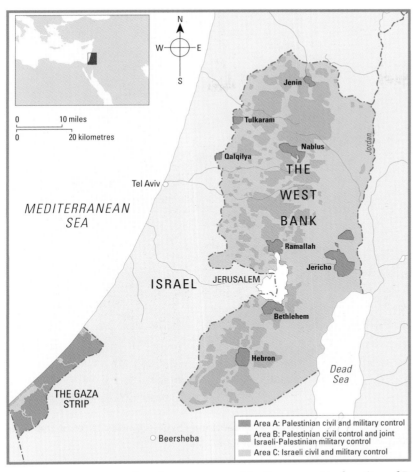

The new distribution of territory as agreed in the Oslo Accords. Under this interim agreement, the West Bank was divided into three areas: Area A was placed under full Palestinian control; Area B was placed under joint Palestinian-Israeli control; and Area C remained under full Israeli control.

Following the signing of the Gaza-Jericho agreement in May 1994, Israeli troops hand over control of their Gaza City base to the Palestinian Authority.

between two Israeli academics and a PLO delegation. The talks had no official status, although they were conducted with the knowledge and approval of Yossi Beilin, Israel's deputy prime minister. During these talks, the PLO delegation adopted a surprisingly flexible position, in contrast to their attitude at the official talks in Washington. This attitude, plus Rabin's realization that the real terrorist threat was now coming from the Islamist groups and not the PLO, persuaded him to reverse Israel's refusal to negotiate with the PLO. Soon the Israeli delegation was upgraded to include senior government officials.

Together they worked out a 'Declaration of Principles', which has become the foundation of peace negotiations between Israel and the Palestinians ever since. The Declaration of Principles stated that Israel and the PLO recognized each other's legitimacy, and that Israel would start to withdraw from the occupied territories over a five-year period, beginning with the Gaza Strip and Jericho. A Palestinian Authority (PA) was formed from the PLO with limited powers of self-rule in the occupied territories.

The document that resulted from these talks, known as the Oslo Accords, was signed at a Washington ceremony hosted by US president Bill Clinton on 13 September 1993. During the ceremony, Yasser Arafat, leader of the PLO, and Yitzhak Rabin, Israeli prime minister, shook hands.

In May 1994, Israel and the PLO signed the Gaza-Jericho agreement in Cairo, which led to the establishment of the PA. That month, Israeli forces withdrew from Jericho and most of the Gaza Strip. In November, Rabin handed new powers to the PA, including responsibility for taxation, health, transport and social services. The following October, Israeli

forces began a phased withdrawal from most of the West Bank. In January 1996, Yasser Arafat was elected president of the PA.

THE PEACE PROCESS STALLS

Despite these positive developments, not everyone welcomed the peace process. Militant groups like Hamas were not prepared to recognize Israel under any circumstances, and many ordinary Palestinians were worried that the Oslo Accords did not guarantee the ultimate setting-up of a Palestinian state. On the Israeli side, many were concerned that the lands they had fought for would be returned to the Palestinians with no real promise of security in return.

The carrying out of the Oslo Accords took place against a background of increasing terrorist violence against Israel from Hamas, Islamic Jihad, and a Lebanese-based Shi'ite group called Hezbollah. As more Israelis were killed, popular opinion shifted towards a more hardline approach. Yitzhak Rabin was assassinated in November 1995 by an Israeli extremist opposed to the peace process. In May 1996, a conservative government came to power in Israel, headed by Benjamin Netanyahu, an opponent of the Oslo Accords. Although Netanyahu claimed to support the peace process, his government agreed to expansion

The funeral of Yitzhak Rabin. The Israeli prime minister was a joint winner of the 1994 Nobel Peace Prize for his efforts at promoting peace with the Palestinians. But he was also hated by right-wing Israelis who blamed him for giving away too much.

of Israeli settlements in the occupied territories, which went against the spirit of the agreement.

The USA put pressure on the Israelis to put a stop to settlement building, and to continue with the troop withdrawals. In October 1998, Netanyahu and Arafat signed a new agreement in Washington, known as the Wye Memorandum. Israel agreed to withdraw from an additional 13 per cent of the West Bank in return for a pledge from the Palestinians to crack down on terrorism.

CAMP DAVID II In July 2000, President Clinton invited the new Israeli prime minister Ehud Barak and Yasser Arafat to Camp David to negotiate the final status of the occupied territories and Jerusalem. By this time, Israeli withdrawals had left 40 per cent of the West Bank and 65 per cent of the Gaza Strip under the full or partial control of the PA. Barak insisted that East Jerusalem plus 80 per cent of the land containing the Jewish settlements on the West Bank would remain part of Israel; the rest could be handed over to the PA. This was more than any Israeli leader had previously offered. Arafat, however, insisted on Israeli withdrawal from the vast majority of the occupied territories, including East Jerusalem. No agreement could be reached, yet Barak was nevertheless criticized in Israel for having offered too much.

Benjamin Netanyahu (left) and Yasser Arafat meet with President Clinton at the White House on 15 October 1998. The Wye Memorandum was signed eight days later.

Areas under full or partial Palestinian control, comprising 26 per cent of the West Bank

Additional areas to be handed over by the Israelis, comprising 13 per cent of the West Bank

Areas under partial control of the Palestinians to be designated a Nature Reserve, comprising 3 per cent of the West Bank

A map showing the agreed reallocations of territory under the Wye Memorandum of November 1998. An additional 12 per cent of the West Bank would be transferred from Area C to Area B, and 1 per cent would move from Area C to Area A.

ISRAELI SETTLER POPULATION GROWTH IN THE WEST BANK AND GAZA STRIP: 1972-2001

Year	West Bank (not including East Jerusalem)	Gaza Strip	Total
1972	800	700	1,500
1983	22,800	900	23,700
1989	69,800	3,000	72,800
1992	101,100	4,300	105,400
1995	133,200	5,300	138,500
1998	161,300	6,100	167,400
2001	201,800	6,500	208,300

[Source: Foundation for Middle East Peace]

CHAPTER 7:
THE SECOND INTIFADA AND THE ROAD MAP

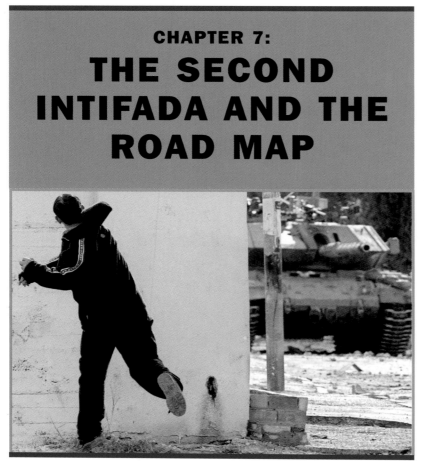

A Palestinian rioter hurls stones at a tank in a West Bank town during the second popular rising, or intifada.

The frustration felt by many Palestinians at the slow progress of the peace process, combined with continuing social and economic hardship, led to renewed violence in the occupied territories in late 2000. The spark for this second intifada came on 28 September when Ariel Sharon, leader of Likud, Israel's most powerful right-wing party, visited Temple Mount, the site of not only the al-Aqsa mosque, a holy Muslim shrine in Jerusalem, but also the Biblical First and Second Temples, sacred to Jews and important to Christians. Sharon was accompanied by around one thousand armed riot police, and some party colleagues. His visit caused widespread protests among Palestinians in Jerusalem, and during these demonstrations Israeli police shot dead six unarmed protestors. Outrage at these killings led to over a month of rioting in the West Bank and Gaza Strip.

The second intifada was led by Islamists and local leaders of Fatah, the largest and most radical faction of the PLO. They demanded total Israeli withdrawal from the occupied territories, removal of all Jewish settlements, the establishment of a sovereign state of Palestine with its capital in Jerusalem, and the right of return of all Palestinian refugees. They were critical of PLO leader Yasser Arafat for offering the Israelis too much in peace negotiations; they also criticized the PA for providing weak leadership and poor services.

Another feature of the second intifada was a rise in suicide bombings and other terrorist attacks inside Israel. These had caused over 160 civilian deaths by April 2002. The organizations which carried out these attacks – Hamas, Islamic Jihad and the al-Aqsa Martyrs Brigade, a militant wing of Fatah – had a more extreme aim: the complete destruction of Israel.

Israel called upon the PA to crack down on the rioters and terrorists of the second uprising, and the PA security forces did occasionally carry out mass arrests of Islamists and members of terrorist organizations. However, the violence continued, and so Israel decided to send its own armed forces into the occupied territories in 2001 to attack the rioters and terrorist bases directly.

In December 2001, Yasser Arafat himself became a target of Israeli anger for his failure to crack down on, and – the Israeli government claimed – his unspoken support for, the terrorists. For the next five months, the PLO leader became a virtual prisoner as Israeli tanks surrounded his presidential compound in the West Bank town

MEDITERRANEAN SEA

9 September 2001, 3 killed — Nahariya

Haifa
2 December 2001, 15 killed

Sea of Galilee

Afula

16 July 2001, 2 killed — Binyamina

Beit She'an

29 November 2001, 3 killed — Hadera

Jenin

7 October 2001, 1 killed
Kibbutz Sheluhot

4 March 2001, 8 killed — Netanya
18 May 2001, 5 killed

Tulkaram

Kfar Saba — Qalqilya — Nablus
22 April 2001, 1 killed — 28 March 2001, 2 killed

Emanuel

1 June 2001, 19 killed — Tel Aviv
14 February 2001, 8 killed — Holon

Ariel

Jordan

THE WEST BANK

Ramallah

9 August 2001, 15 killed
1 December 2001, 11 killed — JERUSALEM

ISRAEL

Beit Sahur

22 June 2001, 2 killed — Dugit
Gaza

Dead Sea

Hebron

THE GAZA STRIP

Legend:
- Location and number of Israelis killed by Palestinians in targeted killings, September 2000–December 2001
- Location of suicide bombings in 2001
- Locations of the main targeted assassinations of terrorist leaders by Israeli forces, July–December 2001

Three bombs carried by two suicide bombers explode in Jerusalem on 1 December 2001, killing at least eight people.

The map shows the locations of terrorist attacks on Israelis, and assassinations of terrorist leaders by Israel, during 2000 and 2001. As attacks on troops and civilians mounted, the Israelis began to target people who were directing the violence.

THE SECOND INTIFADA

(figures apply to the period 29 September 2000–1 June 2003)

Year	Palestinians killed by Israeli security forces	Palestinians killed by Israeli civilians	Israeli civilians killed by Palestinians	Israeli security forces personnel killed by Palestinians
2000	272	6	18	19
2001	454	7	65	21
2002	990	13	88	101
to 1 June 2003	305	6	16	18
TOTAL	**2,021**	**32**	**187**	**159**

[Source: B'tselem, the Israeli Information Center for Human Rights in the Occupied Territories]

of Ramallah. This had the effect of increasing support for Arafat among Palestinian militants.

Between April and June 2002, in response to a wave of suicide bombings, Israeli forces invaded and reoccupied the West Bank towns of Ramallah, Bethlehem, Jenin, Tulkaram, Qalqilya, Nablus and Hebron. PA buildings and suspected terrorist bases were shelled, weapons were confiscated, house-to-house searches were conducted, arrests were made and strict curfews were imposed. The Palestinians claimed the Israelis massacred civilians in Jenin. Israel insisted it had merely responded to organized armed resistance. The UN Security Council demanded that Israel withdraw from the reoccupied West Bank towns without delay.

THE ROAD MAP TO PEACE
In April 2003, a new peace plan, known as the 'road map to peace', was published. Drawn up by the UN, USA,

Water resources on the West Bank. Access to water supplies for Palestinians and Israelis remains an important issue which will need to be resolved before a lasting peace can be achieved.

An Israeli tank, looking for Palestinian militants, blocks access to a refugee camp in Jenin, June 2002.

An Israeli soldier passes a sign protesting at the building of the security fence through a Palestinian village on the West Bank.

European Union and Russia, with Israeli and Palestinian consultation, the plan sought a two-state solution to the conflict: setting up an independent Palestinian state in the occupied territories, alongside Israel. The plan set out to achieve this in three stages by 2005.

The first stage required the following: the end of Palestinian violence; the reform of Palestinian political institutions (which had been accused of corruption, and tacit support of terrorism); the dismantling of all Israeli settlements in the occupied territories constructed since March 2001; progressive Israeli withdrawal from designated areas of the occupied territories. Stage two would involve the creation of an independent Palestinian state. There would also be discussions at this stage on crucial issues such as the sharing of water resources and economic development. At stage three, the parties would reach agreement on final borders, the status of Jerusalem, the return of

Palestinian refugees, and Israeli settlements – leading to a permanent end to the conflict.

Before the plan's publication, Yasser Arafat came under increasing pressure to step down as leader of the PA. His failure to clamp down on terrorism had discredited him in the eyes of many in the international community – although he remained popular with Palestinians. In March 2003, Yasser Arafat appointed a prime minister of the PA. He was Mahmoud Abbas, a strong believer in the peace process, to whom Arafat surrendered many of his powers.

There was progress on the plan in June 2003, when a ceasefire was declared by the terrorist groups, and Israel began to withdraw its forces from the occupied territories and release some Palestinian prisoners. However, any optimism quickly receded when terrorist attacks recommenced in August, and Israeli troops halted their withdrawals and began a campaign of assassinations of top terrorist leaders. On 6 September,

Thirteen kilometres of the security fence will be in the form of a concrete wall (shown here being built) around the town of Qalqilya, and also separating parts of Jerusalem from adjacent Palestinian areas.

Mahmoud Abbas resigned after emerging the loser in a power struggle with Arafat, and having failed to control Palestinian violence. Arafat appointed Ahmed Qureia as his replacement. As suicide bombings continued, Israel vowed to exile – or possibly assassinate – Yasser Arafat.

THE FUTURE While the international community continues to try to promote peace in the region, recent developments on the ground are making the road map, or any similar effort at achieving a two-state solution to the conflict, more and more unlikely. Since April 2003, Israel has begun constructing a 'security fence' around the Palestinian-controlled territories as a means of protecting itself and ending terrorist attacks. There are fears that the six-metre high fence, topped with barbed wire and lined with guard towers, will make any new Palestinian state little more than a reservation, without access to the resources it

needs to form a viable, independent nation.

On the Israeli side of the fence, new houses are being built for Jewish settlements in the West Bank. New roads, telecommunications, electricity and water supplies are binding the settlements ever more closely to the state of Israel. The Israeli people increasingly see these settlements as permanent parts of their country, which cannot be given away during

New homes are built at the Jewish West Bank settlement of Ariel in June 2003, despite international pressure on Israel to stop expanding its settlements.

peace talks. Seeing this, increasing numbers of Palestinians despair of ever achieving an independent state of Palestine. They are starting to believe that their only choice is to accept Israel's control of their land and to demand equal rights.

This one-state solution might not be welcomed by Jewish Israelis, because within a few years, such a state would lose its Jewish majority. There are currently 5.4 million Jews and 4.93 million Arabs in Israel and the occupied territories. It is estimated that by 2020 – due to the higher birth rate of Arabs compared to Jews – there will be 6.69 million Jews and 8.49 million Arabs. With Arabs demanding equal rights and 'one citizen one vote', there may well be pressure on Israel to abandon its Jewish identity. Israel's Jewish community would of course stubbornly resist any such move.

The current state of the Arab-Israeli conflict is marked by periodic moves towards peace followed by sudden outbreaks of

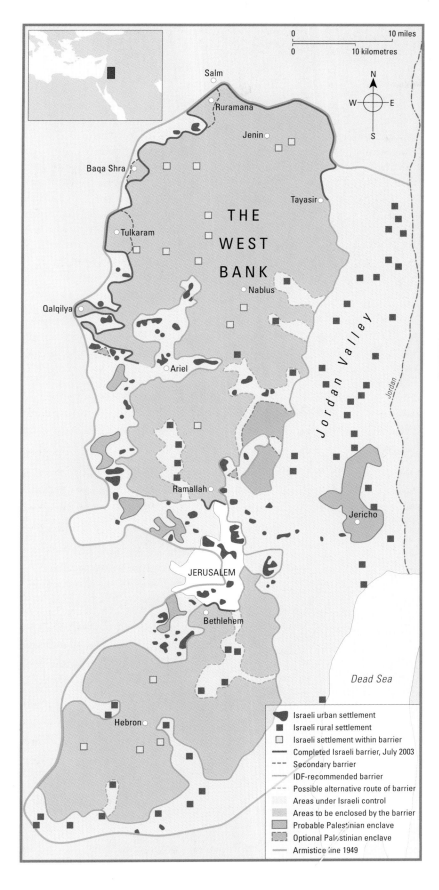

Salm

Ruramana

Jenin

Baqa Shra

Tayasir

□ THE
WEST
BANK

Tulkaram

Nablus

Qalqilya

Jordan Valley

Jordan

Ariel

Ramallah

Jericho

JERUSALEM

Bethlehem

Dead Sea

Hebron

0   10 miles
0   10 kilometres

N
W   E
S

- ■ Israeli urban settlement
- ■ Israeli rural settlement
- □ Israeli settlement within barrier
- —— Completed Israeli barrier, July 2003
- --- Secondary barrier
- —— IDF-recommended barrier
- ~~~ Possible alternative route of barrier
-   Areas under Israeli control
-   Areas to be enclosed by the barrier
-   Probable Palestinian enclave
-   Optional Palestinian enclave
- —— Armistice line 1949

FEAR OF WAR

'As one who participated in all the wars of the state of Israel, I saw the horror of wars. I saw the fear of wars. I saw my best friends being killed in battles. I was seriously injured twice ... I believe I understand the importance of peace, not more but not less than many of the politicians who speak about peace, but never had this experience.'

[Israeli prime minister Ariel Sharon, July 2003]

A map showing the projected route of the security fence in the West Bank. In October 2003, the UN passed a resolution saying the barrier was 'in contradiction to international law'. Despite this, Israeli public opinion is strongly in favour of the fence.

renewed violence, and there seems little prospect of an immediate resolution. However, the region has provided some surprising examples of progress towards peace, such as the treaties between Israel and Egypt in 1979 and Israel and Jordan in 1994. There is always a chance – through international pressure and enlightened leadership – that the parties currently locked in battle might discover a way of sharing the land and resources they are now fighting over, and bring the conflict which began over a century ago to an end.

ABBAS, MAHMOUD (1935-)
Also known as Abu Mazen, Abbas was born in Safad, Palestine. He was a founding member of Fatah and a member of the PLO Executive Committee since 1968. He has headed the PLO Department for National and International Relations since 1980. Abbas is considered a moderate, and is strongly in favour of a peaceful settlement with Israel. He coordinated negotiations during the Madrid conference and the Oslo Accords. Although popular in the international community, Abbas lacks support among ordinary Palestinians. He was prime minister of the PA for just four months in 2003, before being replaced.

ALLON, YIGAL (1918-1980)
An Israeli military commander and politician, Allon was born in Galilee. He was a co-founder in 1941 of the Palmah, a highly trained Zionist commando unit, becoming its commander in 1945. During the 1947-9 War, he commanded the southern front, driving invading Arab armies from Israel. In 1954 he was elected to the Knesset, and from 1961 to 1968 served as Minister of Labour. He became deputy prime minister in 1968, and then Minister of Education and Culture. From 1974 to 1977, he was Foreign Minister.

ARAFAT, YASSER (1929-)
The future leader of the PLO was born in Gaza. In 1958, he met fellow Palestinian activist Abu Jihad. He then moved to Jerusalem where he founded Fatah in 1959. Arafat was elected chairman of the PLO in 1969. After the PLO's clash with Jordan in 1971, he moved to Lebanon and remained there until

besieged by the Israeli army in 1982, after which he moved to Tunisia. During the 1970s and 1980s, Arafat gradually changed the PLO from a terrorist group into an organization resembling a government-in-exile, committed to seeking a peaceful settlement with Israel. In 1993 he signed the Oslo Accords with Israel, returning to the occupied territories in 1994, and in 1996 he was elected president of the PA. Since then he has increasingly been seen by Israel and the USA as an obstacle to peace because of his refusal to condemn Palestinian militants. He was placed under house arrest between December 2001 and April 2002, and in 2003 the Israeli government threatened him with permanent exile. Yet he remains a popular figure among Palestinians.

ASAD, HAFIZ (1930-2000)
Asad was born at Qardaha in Syria. In 1964 he entered the Syrian government, and rose to become leader of a faction of the ruling Ba'ath Party. That faction siezed power in 1970, and Asad became President of Syria, a post he held until his death.

ASHWARI, HANAN (1946-)
A Palestinian academic and politician who became official spokeswoman for the Palestinian delegation during the peace conferences of 1991 to 1993. She promoted a moderate and reasonable image of the Palestinian cause to the West. Ashwari was elected as an independent to the Palestinian Legislative Council in 1996.

BAKER, JAMES (1930-)
As US Secretary of State from 1989 to 1992, Baker worked hard at

promoting a peaceful settlement to the conflict. In March 1991, he became the first American Secretary of State to meet with a Palestinian delegation. His attempts at setting up a general Middle East peace conference were impeded by Israel's insistence that it would only conduct bilateral talks with individual Arab states.

BALFOUR, ARTHUR JAMES (1848-1930)
As British foreign secretary from 1916 to 1919, Balfour proclaimed British support for the setting up of a Jewish state in Palestine in the famous Balfour Declaration of 1917. Balfour had previously served as prime minister from 1902 to 1905.

BARAK, EHUD (1942-)
Born in Kibbutz Mishmar Hasharon, Barak joined the IDF in 1959 and served in various positions of command in the 1967, 1973 and 1982 wars. In April 1991 he was appointed Chief of the General Staff and was promoted to Lieutenant General, the highest rank in the Israeli military. Barak oversaw the IDF's redeployment in Gaza and Jericho following the May 1994 agreement, and he played a major role in the peace treaty with Jordan. Elected as a member of the Labor Party to the Knesset in 1996, he served as prime minister and minister of defence from May 1999 to February 2001.

BEGIN, MENACHEM (1913-1992)
A passionate Zionist from an early age, Begin was born in Brest-Litovsk (in present-day Belarus). In the 1930s he lived in eastern Europe, fighting on behalf of Jews, and arranging for their immigration to Palestine. In the

1940s he joined the Jewish terrorist organization Irgun, organizing various attacks on the British. From 1948, Begin was a right-wing opposition party leader in the Knesset, and in 1977 he was elected prime minister. He helped initiate the peace process with Egypt which led to the 1979 Israel-Egypt Peace Treaty. Begin's government launched Operation Peace for Galilee, Israel's invasion of Lebanon, in 1982.

BEN-GURION, DAVID (1886-1973)

Israel's first prime minister, Ben-Gurion was born in Plonsk, Poland, and was a leader of a Zionist youth group in his teens. He moved to Palestine in 1906 and helped set up the first kibbutz (an agricultural workers' commune). In 1935 he was elected chairman of the World Zionist Organization, and was a prominent leader in the struggle to establish the state of Israel. In May 1948 he became prime minister and defence minister of the new state, and oversaw the establishment of Israel's institutions, the development of new towns, and the settlement of outlying areas. He also led Israel during the 1956 Suez War, finally resigning as prime minister in 1963.

BUSH, GEORGE HERBERT WALKER (1924-)

As president of the USA from 1989 to 1993, George Bush organized a coalition of Western and Arab states which combined to defeat Saddam Hussein's Iraq in the 1991 Gulf War. Out of gratitude for Arab support in the Gulf War, Bush placed pressure on Israel to participate in a general Middle East peace conference.

BUSH, GEORGE WALKER (1946-)

The 43rd president of the USA was elected in 2000. Following the 11 September terrorist attacks on the USA, Bush declared war on terrorism. Islamist terror groups such as Al Qaeda, Hezbollah and Hamas – and the countries which supported them – became targets in this new kind of war. In April 2003, Bush threw his weight behind a new attempt to end the Arab-Israeli conflict, authorizing the publication of the 'road map to peace'.

CARTER, JIMMY (1924-)

As president of the USA from 1977 to 1981, Carter was instrumental in mediating the Egypt-Israel Peace Treaty of 1979. Although a committed supporter of Israel, Carter believed that the Palestinians should have a homeland and be compensated for the losses they had suffered. He invited Begin and Sadat to the presidential lodge at Camp David for a conference which lasted from 4 to 17 September 1978, a meeting which led to the peace treaty, signed the following year.

CLINTON, BILL (1946-)

As US president from 1993 to 2001, Bill Clinton worked tirelessly to promote peace in the Middle East. In 1993 he hosted the signing of the Declaration of Principles on the White House lawn in Washington. The Clinton administration encouraged bilateral talks between Israel and Jordan that led to the signing of the July 1994 Washington Declaration. A new diplomatic push for peace was led by Clinton in 1998, leading to the Wye Memorandum, signed by Arafat and Netanyahu in October. In July 2000, Clinton hosted a Camp David Peace Summit between Barak and Arafat, which ended without agreement.

DAYAN, MOSHE (1915-1981)

Born in Galilee, Dayan was just fourteen when he joined the Haganah, a Jewish underground organization that defended Jewish settlements from Arab attacks. In 1941, he joined the British army in the Middle East, and lost his left eye during a battle in Lebanon. During the 1947-9 War, Dayan led the defence of Jewish settlements in the Jordan Valley and helped to defeat Egyptian forces in the south. In the 1950s, he organized raids on Arab positions in Gaza and elsewhere, and led Israel's Suez campaign in 1956. In 1959 he entered the Knesset and served as Minister of Agriculture from 1959 to 1964, and then as Minister of Defence from 1967 to 1974. It was Dayan who persuaded the Israeli government to launch the pre-emptive strike that began the Six-Day War. He was also blamed for Egypt's surprise attack in 1973, leading to his resignation. As foreign minister between 1977 and 1979, Dayan was instrumental in negotiating the Camp David Accords with Egypt.

EBAN, ABBA (1915-2002)

An Israeli diplomat and politician. As foreign minister, Eban worked to maintain Israel's good relations with the USA and establish its assocation with the European Community. During the 1960s, Eban fought for Israel's cause at the United Nations.

ESHKOL, LEVI (1895-1969)

Born in Oratovo in the Ukraine, Eshkol joined a Zionist group as a youth and came to Palestine at 19. In 1940, he joined the Haganah and in 1947 he helped to establish the IDF. He served as ministers of agriculture and finance, obtaining funds to develop the country and equip the army, before becoming prime minister in 1963. He died in office. He is widely credited with having provided the IDF with the funding and equipment necessary to win the 1967 war.

HERZL, THEODOR (1860-1904)

The founder of the Zionist movement was born in Budapest,

Hungary. As a student in Vienna, and later as a journalist in Paris, he was appalled by the anti-semitism he encountered. Herzl believed that anti-semitism would always be a factor in society, and the only solution for Jews was their mass emigration to a land they could call their own. In 1896, he published *The Jewish State* in which he expanded on this idea. Herzl formed the Zionist Organization and collected funds from Jews around the world to help realize his dream. In 1897, the First Zionist Congress was held at Basle, Switzerland. By the time of his death Zionism had become a mass movement. His remains were brought to Israel in 1949 and reinterred on Mount Herzl in Jerusalem.

HUSSEIN, KING OF JORDAN (1935-1999)

Born in Amman, King Hussein bin Talal assumed the throne of Jordan in 1952. Throughout his 47-year-reign he struggled to promote peace in the Middle East. After the 1967 war, he helped draft UN Resolution 242 calling on Israel to withdraw from the occupied territories in exchange for peace. In 1991, he played an important role in bringing about the Madrid Peace Conference, providing the means for Palestinians to negotiate their future, and also negotiating Jordan's own peace treaty with Israel.

HUSSEIN, SADDAM (1937-)

The ruthless dictator of Iraq came to power in 1979 with ambitions to make Iraq the regional superpower. In 1980 he invaded Iran, beginning an eight-year war that ended in stalemate, and in 1990 he invaded Kuwait. A US-led coalition defeated Iraq and forced its retreat from Kuwait in the 1991 Gulf War. His regime was overthrown by coalition forces in the second Gulf War in 2003, and Hussein fled to an unknown destination. In

December 2003 he was captured by US Special Forces and held in custody pending his future trial.

JIHAD, ABU (1935-1988)

Co-founder with Arafat of Fatah in 1959, Jihad became the military chief of Fatah in the 1960s. He established PLO relations with Jordan, Syria and Saudi Arabia, and organized the Palestinian resistance in the occupied territories. A close ally of Arafat and appointed his official deputy in 1980, Jihad was assassinated by Israeli agents in 1988.

KISSINGER, HENRY (1923-)

As Secretary of State under US presidents Nixon and Ford, Kissinger guided US foreign policy from 1969 to 1975. He played an important role in negotiating a ceasefire in the Middle East after the 1973 war, and was awarded the 1973 Nobel Peace Prize.

MEIR, GOLDA (1898-1978)

Born in Russia and educated in the USA, Meir emigrated to Palestine in 1921. She was active in the struggle against the British and served in various government ministries after 1948. In 1965 she helped to form the Israel Labour Party, and became prime minister in 1969. She accepted blame for Israel's lack of preparation in the 1973 war, and resigned in 1974.

MUBARAK, MUHAMMAD HOSNI (1928-)

The president of Egypt since 1981 began his career in the Air Force. In 1975 he was appointed vice president, and assumed the presidency after Sadat's assassination. Mubarak oversaw the handing back of the last third of Sinai in April 1982, and has sought to maintain peaceful relations with Israel. He aligned Egypt with the coalition forces in the 1991 Gulf War, and has dealt harshly with Islamist opposition groups in

Egypt, leading to an attempt on his life in 1995.

NASSER, GAMAL ABDEL (1918-1970)

The future Egyptian president came to power as leader of a revolutionary group from within the Egyptian army called the Free Officers, who overthrew the king in 1952. Nasser was officially elected president in 1956. Nasser hoped to modernize Egypt by building the Aswan Dam which would allow more of Egypt's land to be brought under cultivation, as well as generate more electricity for the country, and allow water to be stored for times of drought; but after the USA cancelled the loan, he nationalized the Suez Canal, hoping to raise funds that way. The Suez War of 1956 made Nasser a hero in the Arab world. He formed the United Arab Republic with Syria in 1958, but the union was dissolved in 1961 after a coup in Syria. After defeat in the 1967 war, Nasser resigned, but the people took to the streets, demanding his return to government.

NETANYAHU, BENJAMIN (1949-)

Born in Tel Aviv and educated in the USA, Netanyahu returned to Israel in 1967 and enlisted in the IDF, serving in an elite anti-terror unit and achieving the rank of captain. Since 1979 he has organized conferences and written books on countering international terrorism. He served as Israeli ambassador to the UN during the 1980s. In 1988, Netanyahu was elected to the Knesset as a Likud member and was appointed deputy foreign minister. In 1993 he became Likud Party Chairman and served as prime minister from 1996 to 1999, during which time he was accused of hindering the peace process by allowing Jewish settlement building to continue.

PERES, SHIMON (1923-)
Born in Poland, Peres moved to Palestine in 1934, where he joined the Haganah in 1947. From 1953 to 1959 he served as Director General of the Defence Ministry, developing Israel's aircraft industry and nuclear program. In 1959 he was elected to the Knesset, and has remained a member ever since, serving in various ministries, including prime minister from 1984 to 1986 and from 1995 to 1996. During the 1990s, Peres worked hard to maintain the momentum of the peace process and shared the Nobel Peace Prize in 1994.

RABIN, YITZHAK (1922-1995)
Rabin was born in Jerusalem, and served in the Palmach (Jewish commando unit) and then the IDF for 27 years. After his retirement from the military in 1968 he was appointed Israeli ambassador to the USA. In 1973 he was elected to the Knesset and served as prime minister from 1974 to 1977. He focused on improving the economy and strengthening the IDF, and in 1975 he concluded the interim peace agreement with Egypt. Rabin was elected prime minister again in 1992, and made the decision to negotiate directly with the PLO. In 1993 he and Arafat signed the Declaration of Principles in Washington; the following year he signed the Gaza-Jericho Agreement and the Israel-Jordan peace treaty, and shared the Nobel Peace Prize. On 4 November 1995, Rabin was assassinated by a Jewish extremist in Tel Aviv.

REAGAN, RONALD (1911-)
As US president from 1981 to 1989, Reagan was a strong supporter of Israel, and believed in maintaining Israeli military superiority in the Middle East. Under his presidency, the USA initiated various Middle East peace plans, including the Reagan Plan and the Schultz Plan (named after US Secretary of State George Schultz).

SADAT, ANWAR (1918-1981)
Sadat served as Nasser's public relations minister and trusted deputy from 1952. Yet he was fairly unknown when he became president of Egypt in 1970. He quickly proved a bold and decisive leader, offering Israel a peace treaty in return for the Sinai lands, and expelling Soviet advisers when the USSR proved an unreliable ally. Meanwhile he secretly planned a surprise attack on Israel to retake the Sinai after his peace initiatives were rebuffed, which was carried out in October 1973. Egyptian forces were soon repelled, but Sadat's move had created a new momentum for a peace settlement, which he accelerated with a visit to Israel in 1977. This led to the Camp David Accords and the eventual peace treaty with Israel in 1979. Sadat won the Nobel Peace Prize for his efforts, but his recognition of Israel aroused popular anger among Islamists at home, and he was assassinated by Muslim fundamentalists in 1981.

SHAMIR, YITZHAK (1915-)
Born in Poland, Shamir came to Palestine in 1935, and joined the Jewish terrorist organization, Irgun, directed against the British occupation, and later the Stern Gang, a militant faction of Irgun. After independence, Shamir joined Mossad, the Israeli intelligence service, and was elected to the Knesset in 1973 as a member for Likud. He became foreign minister in 1980 before becoming prime minister from 1983 to 1984. Shamir was a hardliner, who opposed Israel's peace treaty with Egypt and the withdrawal from Lebanon. He softened his stance when he returned to office in 1990, agreeing not to respond to Iraq's Scud missile strikes, and taking part in the Madrid peace talks. He stepped down from the Likud leadership in 1993.

SHARON, ARIEL (1928-)
Sharon, born in Kfar Malal, joined the Haganah aged 14, and commanded an infantry company in the 1947-9 war. In 1953 he led the '101' special commando unit that carried out border raids, and commanded a paratroop corps in the 1956 war. In the 1967 and 1973 wars he was commander of an armoured division, and in the latter conflict he led the crossing of the Suez Canal which brought victory. He was elected to the Knesset in 1973 and again in 1977, serving as agriculture and defence minister in the Begin administration. He organized the 1982 invasion of Lebanon, and resigned when he was found indirectly responsible for the massacre at Sabra and Shatila refugee camps in west Beirut. He continued in government, serving in various ministries, before becoming Likud party leader in 1999. He became prime minister in 2001, and was reelected in 2003.

WEIZMANN, CHAIM (1874-1952)
Born in Russia, Weizmann became active in the Zionist movement whilst studying in Europe. His scientific assistance to the Allies during World War I brought him into close contact with British leaders, giving him crucial influence over British policy towards Palestine, and the issuing of the Balfour Declaration in 1917 is partly attributed to Weizmann. In 1920 he became president of the World Zionist Organization, and played a key role in the adoption of the partition plan by the UN in 1947 and in the recognition of Israel by the USA. Weizmann served as the first President of Israel from 1948 until his death four years later.

SIGNIFICANT DATES

1890s
Beginning of Zionist movement.

1900s
Clashes between Palestinians and Jewish settlers.

1917
Balfour Declaration.

1921
Start of British Mandate.

29 NOVEMBER 1947
UN General Assembly votes to accept partition plan.

DECEMBER 1947
War between Palestinian Arabs and Jews begins.

1 APRIL 1948
Zionist offensive begins.

15 MAY 1948
British Mandate ends. Zionist leaders declare the founding of the state of Israel.

16-17 MAY 1948
Neighbouring Arab states invade.

11 JUNE-8 JULY 1948
UN-negotiated ceasefire.

8-18 JULY 1948
Israeli offensives capture many new towns, enlarging Israeli territory.

18 JULY-15 OCTOBER 1948
UN-negotiated ceasefire. Israel establishes itself in newly conquered territory.

1948-9
726,000 Palestinian Arabs become refugees.

FEBRUARY-JULY 1949
Armistice agreements signed by Israel and the Arab states.

JULY 1956
Nasser nationalizes the Suez Canal.

29 OCTOBER 1956
Israel invades Gaza Strip and Sinai Peninsula.

31 OCTOBER 1956
Britain and France launch joint attack on Egypt.

6 NOVEMBER 1956
British and French agree to ceasefire under pressure from USA.

22 DECEMBER 1956
Anglo-French troops evacuated.

MARCH 1957
Israel withdraws from Sinai and Gaza.

AUGUST 1963
Israel begins implementing its National Water Carrier Plan, leading to a near-conflict with Syria.

1964
Formation of PLO.

APRIL-MAY 1967
Border clashes between Israel and Syria.

18 MAY 1967
Nasser demands the evacuation of UN peacekeeping forces, and remilitarizes Sinai.

21 MAY 1967
Nasser closes the Straits of Tiran.

30 MAY 1967
Egypt and Jordan sign a mutual defence treaty.

5 JUNE 1967
Israel launches an aerial attack on Egypt's airfields, virtually destroying the Egyptian Air Force on the ground, followed by a ground invasion of Gaza and Sinai. Jordanian and Syrian armies begin shelling Israeli positions. Israel destroys the Jordanian and most of the Syrian Air Forces.

6 JUNE 1967
Israel captures Ramallah and Jenin.

7 JUNE 1967
Israel captures East Jerusalem and Nablus.

8 JUNE 1967
Israel completes its reconquest of Gaza, Sinai and the West Bank.

9 JUNE 1967
Israel launches invasion of Golan Heights.

10 JUNE 1967
Israel completes conquest of Golan Heights. Ceasefire agreed.

NOVEMBER 1967
UN Security Council adopts Resolution 242 calling on Israel to withdraw from territories seized in June.

1970-1
PLO driven from Jordan and forced into southern Lebanon.

FEBRUARY 1971
Sadat offers peace with Israel in return for Israeli withdrawal from Sinai.

6 OCTOBER 1973
Egypt and Syria launch joint invasion of Israel.

11 OCTOBER 1973
Syrian forces pushed back to their own frontier.

16/17 OCTOBER 1973
Israeli forces cross Suez Canal,

cutting off supplies to Egyptian armies in Sinai.

20 OCTOBER 1973
Ceasefire agreed between Egypt and Israel.

22 OCTOBER 1973
Ceasefire agreed between Syria and Israel.

5 MARCH 1974
Israeli forces withdraw from west bank of Suez Canal.

31 MAY 1974
UN peacekeeping force established on Golan Heights.

SEPTEMBER 1975
Israel withdraws most of its troops from Sinai and a UN-policed buffer zone is placed between Egyptian and Israeli forces.

NOVEMBER 1977
Sadat visits Israel in efforts to secure peace.

MARCH 1978
Operation Litani launched: Israel invades southern Lebanon to attack PLO bases there.

JUNE 1978
Israeli forces withdraw from southern Lebanon.

SEPTEMBER 1978
Israel-Egypt discussions take place at Camp David, USA.

6 JUNE 1982
Operation Peace for Galilee launched: Israel launches full-scale invasion of Lebanon.

13 JUNE 1982
Siege of Beirut begins.

9-10 JUNE 1982
Israeli Air Force destroys Syrian missile batteries in Bekaa Valley, and inflicts defeat on Syrian Air Force in large-scale air battle.

11 JUNE 1982
Ceasefire agreed between Israel and Syria.

12 AUGUST 1982
Siege of Beirut ends when a ceasefire is agreed, and arrangements are made for PLO fighters to be evacuated from Lebanon.

JUNE 1985
Israel withdraws from most of Lebanon, maintaining a 8 km-wide security zone along border.

8 DECEMBER 1987
Start of first intifada.

NOVEMBER 1988
PLO recognizes the state of Israel.

2 AUGUST 1990
Saddam Hussein's Iraq invades Kuwait.

16 JANUARY 1991
Gulf War begins

JANUARY-FEBRUARY 1991
39 Scud missiles launched at Israel.

27 FEBRUARY 1991
Gulf War ends. Kuwait is liberated.

OCTOBER 1991
Middle East peace conference held in Madrid.

JULY 1992
Discussions begin in Oslo between Palestinian and Israeli delegations.

13 SEPTEMBER 1993
Oslo Accords signed in Washington. End of first intifada.

MAY 1994
Israel and the PLO sign the Gaza-Jericho agreement in Cairo.

OCTOBER 1994
Israeli forces begin phased withdrawal from most of the West Bank.

NOVEMBER 1995
Israeli prime minister Yitzhak Rabin is assassinated.

JANUARY 1996
Yasser Arafat elected president of the PA.

OCTOBER 1998
Wye Memorandum signed in Washington by Arafat and Netanyahu.

MAY 2000
Israeli forces withdraw completely from Lebanon.

JULY 2000
Barak and Arafat meet at Camp David for final status negotiations. Talks end in deadlock.

28 SEPTEMBER 2000
Second intifada begins when Ariel Sharon visits Temple Mount, sparking widespread protests.

DECEMBER 2001
Israeli tanks surround Arafat's headquarters in Ramallah, keeping him a virtual prisoner.

APRIL-JUNE 2002
Israeli forces invade and reoccupy seven West Bank towns in order to destroy terrorist infrastructure.

MARCH 2003
Mahmoud Abbas appointed Palestinian prime minister.

APRIL 2003
'Road map to peace' published, a new internationally backed plan to bring peace to the Middle East by 2005. Israel begins building its 'separation fence' between Palestinian-controlled areas and Jewish settlements on the West Bank.

6 SEPTEMBER 2003
Abbas resigns as prime minister.

activist Someone who takes action in pursuit of a political aim.

air superiority Control of the skies during a military conflict.

annex To take over territory and incorporate it into a state.

anti-semitism Prejudice against Jews.

Arab League A league of Arab states formed in 1944.

armistice A truce in a war to discuss terms for peace.

autonomy Political independence and self-government.

beachhead A part of an enemy shoreline that troops have captured and are using as a base for launching an attack further inland.

besiege Surround a place such as a city with armed forces in order to bring about its capture or surrender.

bilateral negotiations Talks involving two parties or countries.

blockade An organized action using ships and troops designed to prevent people or goods leaving a place.

boycott To cease to deal with something, such as a country, or to stop buying certain goods, as a form of protest.

brigades Large units of an army.

bridgehead A forward position seized by advancing troops in enemy territory which serves as a basis for more advances.

buffer zone A neutral area that lies between hostile forces and reduces the risk of conflict between them.

civil disobedience The deliberate breaking of the law by ordinary citizens, carried out as a non-violent protest.

civilian An ordinary citizen, as opposed to a member of the armed forces.

coalition The temporary union of two or more groups for a particular end, such as a campaign or period of government.

compatriot A person from the same country.

conservative Describing a political or religious outlook that desires to keep things as they are, and to preserve traditional ways of life and behaviour.

curfew An official restriction on people's movements, requiring them to stay indoors for specified periods.

demilitarized zone An area of land between two hostile states where – by mutual or international agreement – neither side is permitted to place its forces.

DFLP The Democratic Front for the Liberation of Palestine is a communist organization, set up in 1969 when it split from the PFLP. It is a member of the PLO, and believes that Palestinian national goals can only be achieved through a revolution of the masses.

division A self-contained military unit in an army capable of sustained operations.

Druze A member of a religious community similar to Islam and found mainly in Israel, Lebanon and Syria.

ethnic Relating to a group with distinctive cultural traits.

exodus A departure from a place that involves large numbers of people.

faction A group existing within a larger group that holds views not always in agreement with the larger group.

Fatah A Palestinian nationalist group founded in 1957 by Yasser Arafat. Fatah became the PLO's leading faction in 1969. It maintains several espionage and terrorist groups within the occupied territories, including Force 17 and the Al-Aqsa Martyrs' Brigade.

Gaza Strip A narrow strip of land on the coast of the eastern Mediterranean, which has been occupied by Israel since 1967, although partial control has been handed over to the Palestinian Authority since 1994.

Haganah A Jewish underground militia that operated between 1920 and 1948, set up to defend Jewish settlements in Palestine from Arab attack.

Holocaust The systematic extermination of nearly six million Jews by the Nazis during World War II.

IAF Israeli Air Force.

IDF Israeli Defence Force.

infrastructure The basic organization of a group which enables it to operate, including its communications systems and its methods of recruitment, finance and obtaining supplies.

intelligence reports Information on secret plans or activities, especially those of foreign governments.

intifada The Palestinian popular uprising in the occupied territories that took place between 1987 and 1993. A second intifada began in September 2000.

Islamist Someone who follows a strict form of Islam based on a literal interpretation of the Koran and other holy Islamic scriptures.

kibbutz A commune in Israel, especially for farming, and dedicated to the principle that production work and domestic work are of equal value.

Knesset The legislative assembly of Israel.

legitimacy The quality of being legitimate, which means conforming to the law or to recognized principles or accepted rules and standards.

lobby Attempt to persuade an influential person, group or government to support a particular cause.

mandate An official command or instruction from an authority. The territories that were placed by the League of Nations under the control of the European powers after World War I were known as mandates or mandated territories.

Maronite Christians Members of a Uniate church, based chiefly in Lebanon. Uniate churches belong to the Eastern Christian tradition, but submit to the authority of the Pope.

mediator Somebody who works with both sides in a dispute in an attempt to help them reach an agreement.

Middle East The region stretching from the eastern Mediterranean to the western side of the Indian subcontinent, including Egypt, the Arabian Peninsula, Israel, Jordan, Lebanon, Syria, Turkey, Iran and Iraq.

militant Extremely active in support of a cause, often to an extent that causes conflict with other people or institutions.

militia A group of people who arm themselves and carry out military operations on behalf of a cause or non-national organization.

multilateral negotiations Talks involving more than two parties or countries.

nationalism Belief in the right of one's people to exist as a nation, or belief in the status of one's nation above all others.

nationalize To transfer a business or industry from private to governmental control.

Nazi Party The National Socialist Party that came to power in Germany under Adolf Hitler in 1933.

Occupied Territories Those areas conquered by Israel in the 1967 Six Day War, including the West Bank and the Gaza Strip, the status of which remain disputed.

Ottoman Empire A Turkish empire established in the late thirteenth century in Asia Minor, eventually extending through the Middle East, which came to an end in 1922.

PA The Palestinian Authority is a Palestinian-run institution with limited powers of government over the Palestinians in the West Bank and Gaza Strip. It was established in 1994 as part of the 1993 Oslo Accords between the PLO and Israel.

partition The division of a country into two or more separate states.

PFLP The Popular Front for the Liberation of Palestine is a left-wing Palestinian nationalist organization, founded in 1967, which joined the PLO in 1968.

PLO Originally founded in 1964, the Palestinian Liberation Organization is an organization of Palestinian Arabs dedicated to the establishment of an independent Palestinian state in the West Bank, Gaza and possibly parts or all of Israel.

PPP The Palestine People's Party was founded in 1947 as the National Liberation League before changing its name to the Palestine Communist Party and finally to the PPP. The party is a communist faction within the PLO.

pre-emptive strike An attack carried out on an enemy before the enemy has had a chance to strike first.

prejudice (noun): Fear, hatred or mistrust of a person or group, based on ignorance and irrational feelings; (verb): to cause harm or disadvantage to a person or group.

radar station A military installation employing radar – a method of identifying the position of distant objects using radio waves.

reconnaissance The exploration of an area, especially to gather intelligence about the strength and positioning of enemy forces.

refugee Someone who is seeking refuge, especially from war or persecution, by going to a foreign country.

regime A particular government, especially one regarded as harsh or cruel.

reservation An area of land set aside for a particular purpose. In North America the term has been used to describe areas of land for the use of Native North American people. Some Palestinians see parallels between this and their own situation once the separation fence has

been built.

Scud missile A type of surface-to-surface missile.

secular Not concerned with religious matters.

settlement A new community built in a place that is unpopulated or populated by people of a different race or ethnic group.

Shi'ite A follower of the Shia branch of Islam, which considers Ali, a relative of Muhammad, and his descendents to be Muhammad's true successors.

sovereign territory An area or region legitimately controlled by a government.

Soviet Union Also known as the USSR (Union of Soviet Socialist Republics), a country formed from the territories of the Russian Empire in 1917, which lasted until 1991.

strafe Attack an enemy on the ground with machine-gun or cannon fire from a low-flying aircraft.

suicide bombing A bomb attack in which a person deliberately allows him or herself to be killed in the process of attempting to destroy something or to kill people.

terrorism The use of violence against civilians and political leaders in order to achieve political aims.

systematic Carried out in an organized and methodical manner.

tacit Understood or implied without being stated openly.

umbrella organization A body that coordinates or protects a number of smaller organizations.

UN General Assembly The main debating body of the United Nations, composed of representatives of all member states.

United Nations An organization of nations, formed in 1945, to promote peace, security, and international cooperation.

UNLU The United National Leadership of the Uprising was the umbrella organization that coordinated the activities of the PLO groups during the first intifada (1987-93).

UN Resolution A decision of the UN reached after a vote of the General Assembly or Security Council.

UNRWA The United Nations Relief and Works Agency provides relief and human services to Palestinian refugees living in the Gaza Strip, the West Bank, Jordan, Lebanon and Syria.

UN Security Council The permanent committee of the United Nations that oversees its peacekeeping operations around the world. Its job is to investigate any dispute or situation that might lead to international friction and to recommend what action should be taken. It calls upon members to apply non-violent measures to prevent or stop aggression. It also has the power to give authorization for military action against an aggressor.

West Bank The region between the Mediterranean Sea and the Jordan River, including the north-west quadrant of the Dead Sea, which does not belong to the state of Israel. Since 1967 the area has been occupied by Israel, although partial control has been handed over to the Palestinian Authority since 1994.

Zionism A worldwide movement that sought to establish a Jewish nation in Palestine. Since 1948, Zionists continue to act in support of Israel.

STATISTICS CONCERNING COMBATANT NATIONS

Casualty Levels

Approximate numbers killed in all the wars fought since 1948:

Israel	12,000
Egypt	24,000
Syria	8,500
Jordan	7,000
Palestinians	7,000 (since 1982)

Distribution of the Palestinian Population and Jewish Settlers in the West Bank and Gaza Since 1967

Year	Palestinians West Bank	Gaza	Jews West Bank & Gaza
1 Dec 1967	604,494	380,800	–
1979	791,000	447,700	3,176 (1976)
1984	896,000	509,900	16,119 (1981)
1988	977,000	588,500	60,500 (1986)
1990	1,075,531	622,016	98,750 (1991)
1997	1,873,476	1,022,207	165,000
2002	1,932,637	1,087,067	226,028

[Source: *Jerusalem Fund for Education and Community Development*; Israeli Central Bureau of Statistics; USAID West Bank and Gaza]

Global Distribution of Palestinian People (1986, 1990/1, 1995 and 2000)

Country	1986	1990/1	1995	2000
Jordan	1,398,050	1,824,179	2,170,101	2,596,986
West Bank/East Jerusalem	951,530	1,075,531	1,227,545	1,383,415
Gaza	545,100	622,016	726,832	837,699
Israel	608,200	730,000	800,755	919,453
Lebanon	271,434	331,757	392,315	463,067
Syria	242,474	301,744	357,881	410,599
Remaining Arab States	582,894	445,195	516,724	599,389
Rest of World	280,846	450,000	500,000	550,000
Total	**4,880,518**	**5,780,422**	**6,692,153**	**7,760,608**

[Source: *Jerusalem Fund for Education and Community Development*]

Jewish Population Distribution in Palestine (1880-1947)

Year	Population Palestinians Numbers (%)	Jews Numbers (%)
1880	300,000 (94)	24,000 (6)
1917	504,000 (90)	56,000 (10)
1922	666,000 (89)	84,000 (11)
1931	850,000 (83)	174,096 (17)
1936	916,061 (72)	384,078 (28)
1945/6	1,242,000 (69)	608,000 (31)
1947 UN Partition	1,300,000 (67)	640,298 (33)

Jewish Land Ownership in Palestine (1880-1947)

Year	Land ownership (cumulative) dunums*	% of land
1880	n/a	n/a
1917	650,000	less than 3
1922	751,192	3
1931	1,171,529	4
1936	1,380,578	5
1945/6	1,588,365	6
1947 UN Partition	1,900,000	7

* 1 dunum = 1,000 square metres

[Source: *Facts and Figures on Palestine* (Washington, DC: Palestine Center, 1991), p.4]

Distribution of Palestinian Refugees Registered with UNRWA (2003)

Region	No. of Camps	Registered Refugees	Registered Refugees in Camps
Jordan	10	1,718,767	304,430
Lebanon	12	391,679	225,125
Syria	10	409,662	119,766
Gaza Strip	8	907,221	478,854
West Bank	19	654,971	176,514
Total	**59**	**4,082,300**	**1,301,689**

[Source: United Nations, *United Nations Relief and Works Agency for Palestine Refugees in the Near East*, 30 June 2003]

FURTHER INFORMATION

RECOMMENDED BOOKS

New Perspectives: Israel and the Arab Nations in Conflict, Nathaniel Harris (Hodder Wayland, 1998)
Troubled World: Arab-Israeli Conflict, Ivan Minnis (Heinemann Library, 2001)
Witness to History: The Arab-Israeli Conflict, Stewart Ross (Heinemann Library, 2004)

SOURCES OF QUOTATIONS

Pages 4-5 Excerpts From Herzl's *The Jewish State*, Jewish Virtual Library, 2003.
Pages 6-7 Quoted in Ritchie Ovendale, *The Origins of the Arab-Israeli Wars* (third edition), Longman, 1999.
Pages 10-11 Quoted in Bard, Mitchell, *Palestinian Refugees*, Jewish Virtual Library, 2003.
Pages 14-15 Israel Ministry of Foreign Affairs.
Pages 16-17 Quoted in Bregman, Ahron and El-Tahri, Jihan, *The Fifty Years War: Israel and the Arabs*, Penguin, 1998.
Pages 20-21 UN Security Council Resolution 242.
Pages 24-5 Quoted in Bregman and El-Tahri.
Pages 26-7 Quoted in Bregman and El-Tahri.
Pages 30-1 Quoted in Marcus, Yoel, *Camp David: The Door to Peace*, Tel Aviv, 1979.
Pages 34-5 Quoted in Wallach, John and Janet, *Arafat in the Eyes of the Beholder*, Random House, 1991.
Pages 38-9 Quoted in Bregman and El-Tahri.
Pages 40-1 Israel Ministry of Foreign Affairs.
Pages 48-9. Quoted on CNN.com: Inside Politics.
Pages 50-1. From an interview by Peter Beaumont, *The Observer*, 13 July 2003.

RECOMMENDED VIDEOS

War and Peace in the Middle East. 3k Media Ltd, 1995. 60 minutes. A study of fifty years of conflict between Arabs and Israelis. The programme includes interviews with Yasser Arafat, Yitzhak Rabin and Shimon Peres.
War Diary: Exodus - The Birth of Israel. Audiovisual Enterprises Ltd, 1989. 52 minutes. Using archive footage, this film shows the events of 1947-8 as the British prepare to withdraw from Palestine and the state of Israel is proclaimed.
Wars in Peace: Six Day War/Yom Kippur War. K-Tel Entertainment, 1992. 80 minutes. Documentary focusing on the Arab-Israeli wars of 1967 and 1973.

RECOMMENDED WEBSITES

http://www.merip.org/palestine-israel_primer/
toc-pal-isr-primer.html
A concise history of the Arab-Israeli conflict from the Middle East Research and Information Project.
http://historyteacher.net/Arab-Israeli_Conflict.htm
A list of links to various websites on Israel and the Palestinians.
http://www.mideastweb.org/briefhistory.htm
A brief history of the Arab-Israeli conflict, told from the Israeli viewpoint.

Note to parents and teachers

Every effort has been made by the publishers to ensure that these websites are suitable for children; that they are of the highest educational value; and that they contain no inappropriate or offensive material. However, because of the nature of the Internet, it is impossible to guarantee that the contents of these sites will not be altered. We strongly advise that Internet access is supervised by a responsible adult.

PLACES TO VISIT

Temple Mount/Haram Al-Sharif The Temple Mount (known to Muslims as Haram Al-Sharif) is a hill in the eastern part of the Jerusalem's Old City, and is the site of two ancient Jewish temples. Since the seventh century, it has also been a place of Muslim worship. It is the world's holiest site for Jews, the third holiest site for Muslims, and also a place of special significance to Christians.
Dome of the Rock This famous Islamic mosque was built between 687 and 691 CE. The rock in the centre of the dome is believed by Muslims to be the spot to which Muhammad was brought by night and from which he ascended through the heavens to God.
Western or Wailing Wall This outer courtyard wall is all that remains of the second Jerusalem Temple, the holiest building in Judaism, destroyed by the Romans around 2,000 years ago. It is a traditional site of prayer for Jews.
Al-Aqsa Mosque The Al-Aqsa Mosque is the largest mosque in Jerusalem, and was completed in 710 CE. It is believed to have been built on the site of the original Jerusalem Temple. The mosque has been the target of attacks by Jewish extremists.

INDEX

Numbers in **bold** refer to captions to pictures or, where indicated, to maps.